THE ART OF MARGOT FONTEYN

Margot Fonteyn [signature]

photographed by KEITH MONEY

with a commentary contributed by

NINETTE DE VALOIS

FREDERICK ASHTON

KEITH MONEY

and

MARGOT FONTEYN *herself*

Dance Books

First published 1965 by
Michael Joseph Ltd.
This edition published 1975 by
DANCE BOOKS LTD.,
9 Cecil Court, London WC2N 4EZ
© *1965, 1975 Keith Money*

ISBN 0 903102 22 6

Printed and bound in Great Britain by
Hazell Watson & Viney Ltd, Aylesbury, Bucks

Introduction
KEITH MONEY

Margot Fonteyn never makes explanations of her work; in one sense she is unable to, and in another sense the entire process of explaining has taken place on stage. This premise one acknowledges and accepts, yet as one probes her thoughts and seeks her opinions one is constantly stimulated by a mind of exceptional clarity and perception. She would consider unnecessary such thoughts of hers as are recorded in this book; they are there because I deem it right that they should appear. The verbatim recordings are from numerous conversations in which she always met my insatiable curiosity with direct answers, despite much tiredness and a natural disinclination to analyse her own work. In fact our discussion of Swan Lake one evening made her realise that she was—for the first time in her life—seeking and discovering a theoretical reasoning for her reading of the dual roles in that ballet; a reading which for the whole of her career had remained entirely instinctive. This book *is* Margot Fonteyn in that she is not only its subject but also its guiding inspiration. The pictures in this book have all found some sort of response in her, as has their positioning on each page, yet her inclination—as in her art—would be a constant sifting and paring away. This I have resisted with mixed feelings; on the one hand realising that a terrible multitude of the photographs do not reveal the full height of her art, and on the other hand realising that a mere handful of near-perfect studies will not even begin to scale the lowest slopes of her astonishing range. The Daphnis and Chloë section in the centre of this book is, I believe, the most deeply satisfactory to her; its echo truest to the ballet nearest her heart. I hope some of the large pictures of this ballet will also give some hint of the exquisitely apt Ashton choreography. In this respect I was anxious to let the ballerina speak at length on "Fred's ballets", that in so doing I might allow the emergence of some clue to her own mental approach, and reaction, to such profoundly beautiful works as Symphonic Variations. Elsewhere, I hope that the random comments may reflect a subtle emphasis, a suggestion of her particular development, when in juxtaposition to certain pictures; and of course both Dame Ninette de Valois and Sir Frederick Ashton speak on the various facets of her earlier career.

If we begin to think of Fonteyn in her greatest roles, it is only with difficulty that the images of each successive character can be made to make way for the next. If we should think first of Ondine then we are led on progressively through the multiple images of *that* role: her first flighty, hesitant steps beyond the waterfall, the flutters of alarm at each new night sound, the astonishment caused by the sight of her own shadow as it follows faithfully beside her along the castle wall; her puzzlement as it vanishes in the empty archway, and then her delight at its recovery behind her. There is the moment when she brushes a wisp of hair away from her cheek and, in so doing, senses that the mocking twin is in fact herself. Each new element of discovery is fresh and mysterious and not pre-ordained, for it is also at the soul of the music; the reaction is not prompted by the music, the music *is* the reaction. If the arms move in space they dispense the musical phrases visually, cool and unadorned by any mannerisms, and spanning onwards with an unbroken thread at their core. Placed along this thread, like perfectly gradated pearls, are the shapes—the arabesques and attitudes—that echo points in time, explaining mathematics and the mysterious laws of astronomy. For an arm extended upwards in an arabesque should strike to the heart of a star's meridian. One can lower an arm by only a hair's breadth from a complementary angle, yet when its echo nears the star it is a hundred thousand miles away from its target. Fonteyn's genius is that she cannot miss her star. A curve described by an arm may need to travel around the world to come back to its point of departure, but return it must. Her art springs from the still centre.

Late at night after the first performance of Ondine, I went home and did several drawings—something I am aware of doing only after very profound and beautiful experiences in ballet. The results as I remember them were totally unsatisfactory, but it was a form of exorcism; laying an image to rest so that I might get some sleep myself. It was probably then that I first felt a nagging desire to snare those pearls—those truths expressed in visual shapes. Photography was obviously the most suitable servant to this aim, but the idea that *I* might turn a camera on ballet did not solidify until almost a full five years later. In the intervening time I merely stored the impressions in my mind and occasionally committed a few to paper. As it happened, it was the figure of Fonteyn in movement that registered itself in the emulsion of my first ballet photograph.

Gradually I became like a lepidopterist trying to snare emotional butterflies; I was miserable and frustrated if I did not somehow pin the mental image as well as the visual image. (This purely private ideal may or may not communicate itself to the onlooker.) My original desire to place a fragment of Fonteyn's art between the covers of a book failed entirely to take into account the fact that here was one ballerina with an almost psychological horror of cameras. Her distrust of the evil little machine with the—to her—deafening click, was presumably the reason for the terrible paucity of action photographs of Fonteyn. However, if she was stubborn I was more so. Rather desperately I fired at her one afternoon a single query: "Well?" She put a forefinger to her cheek, looked at me quizzically and weighed a thousand things in her mind. After a pause she said simply "Yes," in a very small voice. The voyage of discovery had begun.

For the beginning I was elated. Aware too, in the back of my mind, of a rather terrifying responsibility, but nevertheless elated. It was only as I continued to discover my subject as Margot the person, rather than as Fonteyn the prima ballerina, that my inadequacy grew clearer. The strictly obvious description of her character would probably be "a Latin warmth contained within an English reserve." Much too obvious. The most striking characteristics of her personality would seem to be: simplicity, lack of egotism to a quite remarkable degree, loyalty, generosity of spirit, courage, and willpower allied to an astonishing mental discipline which is, on occasions, mistaken for lack of genuine warmth. To her younger working colleagues she can seem basically withdrawn, an enigma behind a brightly bubbling façade. Her immediate gaiety *is* a major feature; beneath it is a very deep wisdom, and at the centre of all that, a rather haunting sadness.

My own strongest images of Margot are not all seen in the frame of a stage proscenium. There is the random memory of her sitting, tired and wan, in the corner of a steamy suburban railway carriage near midnight. Up in the luggage rack there is a large bouquet, and in her hands two drooping posies which had been tossed from the Gallery at Covent Garden less than an hour earlier; tributes to a ballerina who had just given an unforgettable performance in The Sleeping Beauty. Towards the end of the journey, enthusiastic youngsters in black leather jackets make their girl friends break the ice by requesting autographs, before bounding across to enter into an animated conversation themselves. At the destination there are flowers handed out all round. One of the young men looks at his leather jacket, lacking the necessary buttonhole. "Well," he says, "there's nothing for it. Just have to get the old chisel out tonight and make one!" Still later the same evening she is busy in the silent precincts of the country hospital where her husband receives specialist treatment for his spinal injuries. Amidst the clutter of a scullery room, she moves about quietly and organised, with her sleeves pulled to the elbows; unwiring flowers, standing them in water, saving the ribbons, tip-toeing up and down the corridors on small errands.

Up and out again even before the morning papers arrive, she probably never saw that on that particular morning they spoke of: ". . . the magic in watching a great dancer distilling the pure essence of femininity and also touchingly portraying a 16-year-old fairy princess. She was a sublime blend of exquisite dancer, fine actress and lovely woman. She fulfilled the balletic paradox whereby dancing is nothing without style yet style is meaningless until focussed through the prism of a complex and technically prodigious role. . . . the 404th Covent Garden presentation of The Sleeping Beauty was a very memorable Fonteyn occasion. She may repeat it; she can never exceed it." So felt the Daily Telegraph. The Times spoke of her "matchless Aurora" and wondered "whether any ballerina has ever danced it so well." The Daily Mail added "At the risk of being a bore, I can only say it again—Margot Fonteyn's Aurora is an unrivalled gem. . . . she sailed through the difficult Rose Adagio with complete aplomb, impeccable balances and dazzling, youthful charm." And The Guardian concluded ". . . there was a contagious gaiety about her Rose Adagio, a sense of carefree authority, a lovely sense, too, of April youthfulness. We all cherish Fonteyn's Auroras, Odette-Odiles and Giselles nowadays with an almost parental solicitude; an Aurora such as yesterday's is our reward."

Perhaps it was her reward too; the tiredness of having given her utmost. She is a tireless perfectionist, nervous and full of self doubts. It may have been these attributes of hers which gave me the courage to persevere. The failures in this book are my failures; what remains is the result of her inspiration—as a dancer, and as a friend.

The Sleeping Beauty

"In 1938, when Ninette had made the decision to mount The Sleeping Beauty, I was informed that I would dance Aurora. One never dared question the wisdom of such a frightening decision; one simply did as one was told. There was no discussion about precedent or character; the steps all came out of Sergueyev's great long white books in which he would refer to his notation, which only he could read. He had numerous volumes of all the ballets he had written down in Leningrad, and our production was probably more faithful than had been possible with Diaghilev's version in 1921. No quarter was given over the great technical demands of the role. As always, one did exactly as one was told. I could not really do it at all. One of my many difficulties was that I was also very fat at the time—as one can see from looking at old photographs.

"The general success of the production has always seemed strange from my point of view; it has always been the ballet I have least liked, and the character of Aurora seems characterless. In its earliest days I had no feeling for the role. Before working on it I had heard a lot of the music, and one of my first disappointments was to discover that the Grand Pas de Six was not my music at all. I was heartbroken to think that I was not going to be able to dance to that particular section of the score. I was disappointed in the choreography; extremely disappointed in the costumes. In fact I ran home and cried bitterly after seeing the costume designs of that first production, the result of a theory that the Diaghilev version had not succeeded because it was over-dressed. Our costumes were done in a very simple, almost severe way and in the event we were almost as disastrously under-dressed as the Diaghilev version may have been over-dressed. Despite my lack of interest, the ballet must have been an immediate success.

"My other distractions at the time were equally taxing productions of Giselle, Casse Noisette, and the dual role in Swan Lake. I was very inadequate. Always, when told I was going to do one of these big ballets, I would reply: 'Oh but I can't; I'm not ready!' Of course I was right; I am sure that I was not ready. Perhaps just slightly more ready than the others. Two hundred performances later even *I* began to feel my way into The Sleeping Beauty, but there were periods when I went on to the stage and found, to my horror, that the ballet's meaning had completely deserted me; I did not know *why* a particular step should be required. There was no alternative but to battle on. During the War we were doing The Sleeping Beauty a great deal, probably twice a week, then at the end of the War they opened it at Covent Garden. I think one did about three performances a week for something like three months, with three or four of us alternating in the ballet continuously. The Sleeping Beauty was a fantastic success when we opened our first American tour with it, but the preparatory strain had been great. For my own part I was convinced that the American public would not like me anyway. I was not their kind of dancer; I had no great strength or technique. I felt that whatever qualities I *did* have were rather quiet and lyrical, almost subdued, and I was quite sure that this would never appeal to the new audiences. What apparently did surprise them was the exploding of the myth wherein classical ballerinas were thought to have very pale, serious faces accentuated with pale make-up. They had come to associate this with productions of Swan Lake and Les Sylphides. When they were suddenly confronted with me running on to the stage and smiling happily from ear to ear, the sight astonished them. Underneath it I was so nervous I was all but paralysed —like a hypnotised rabbit. For three months before the New York opening nobody had talked about anything else. 'In America we will do this. . . For America we will take that. . .' Everything at home centred on America. A mass hysteria seemed to grip the company and somehow I seemed to be stuck at the centre of it, frozen. All that I can recall of the opening night is my running on stage in Act One and receiving a tremendous burst of applause—something I doubt had happened to me before. I remember that first entrance and I remember finishing the Aurora pas de deux, but I cannot remember anything that came in between, nor have I ever been able to remember. I do recall the applause after the Aurora pas de deux which I did with Bobby (Helpmann). We took about seven curtain calls which, after a pas de deux, was astonishing to us.

"When the ballet was put on after the War, at Covent Garden, it was decided to incorporate certain changes in the choreography of Act III—changes which Diaghilev had made in his production. Now, nearly twenty years later, they have reverted to the old Sergueyev arrangement, with the Awakening at the end of

Act II as it was originally. I have always hated the last Act variation for Aurora more than anything else. During the last two years I have changed some things, as I have always done over the years. I have gone to Preobrajenska and asked her how she did certain things; or worked with Karsavina and asked her how she did them, and I have worked with Volkova and others. Rightly or wrongly I developed a way of doing Sleeping Beauty. It seems funny to me that it is now accepted in the way that it is, with such high regard for certain familiar passages, because there is no valid basis for saying that the way I did it is the right way. When Rudolf came from the Kirov, where they have such a tradition and have done the ballet for so many years, I was very prepared to listen, because I knew that 'my' version—for all that people accept it now—had only arisen from little pieces that I had been able to snatch and glue together. Even with earlier partners I tended to re-work certain passages according to their view. Michael might say 'This moment doesn't make sense to me,' so we would alter it slightly. Doing the ballet over so very many years one has somehow to find fresh ideas; fresh inspiration. With all the big classics I have always asked other people for their views, then I adopt certain points. Perhaps after a year or two years, or even five years, I revert back to what I was doing before because I decide that, after all, I like it better the way I used to do it. The only way one can possibly keep doing a ballet hundreds of times is to leave oneself open to these fresh influences. When I first did the Rose Adagio, I did not do any of those sustained balances; I cannot even remember when they first emerged. Although I never saw Markova do Sleeping Beauty, people described to me how she would maintain marvellous balance while changing hands with the various suitors, so then I started experimenting. The greatest difficulty is to manage to do it without making a great fuss; it is only really valid to attempt it if one can make it seem as easy as getting off a bus.

"In a way I suppose my position in The Sleeping Beauty is a unique one in our time, in that I have had to ferret out the over-all shape entirely by myself. In Russia they have *always* had the example before them of dancers from preceding generations. For people coming after Pamela May and myself in The Sleeping Beauty, there has perhaps been something to watch and to criticise."

Aurora's arabesque

moments from
the Rose Adagio

Sleeping Beauty section
photographed in Coventry,
September 1964

Fonteyn's superlative stagecraft is so secure that it is difficult to pinpoint any aspect of it, though her ability to transfer herself about the stage almost invisibly when the need arises, must surely have been remarked upon. Her way of linking the punctuation points in choreography defies analysis. She is never hurried, always there on the music and never seen 'arriving'. Her accuracy during moments of stage business never falters. There is the moment when Aurora, doing a series of airy turns with Carabosse's spindle, suddenly pricks herself as her hands glance together above her head during a turn. There is a pained start and the spindle jerks from her hand in a high, desperate arc. Yet never once does the somewhat dangerous projectile fail to find the narrow gap between the proscenium arch and the first wing; no clatter distracts our concern at the figure of Aurora examining her finger.

Carabosse's spell takes effect

THE
VISION
SCENE

with David Blair as Prince Florimund

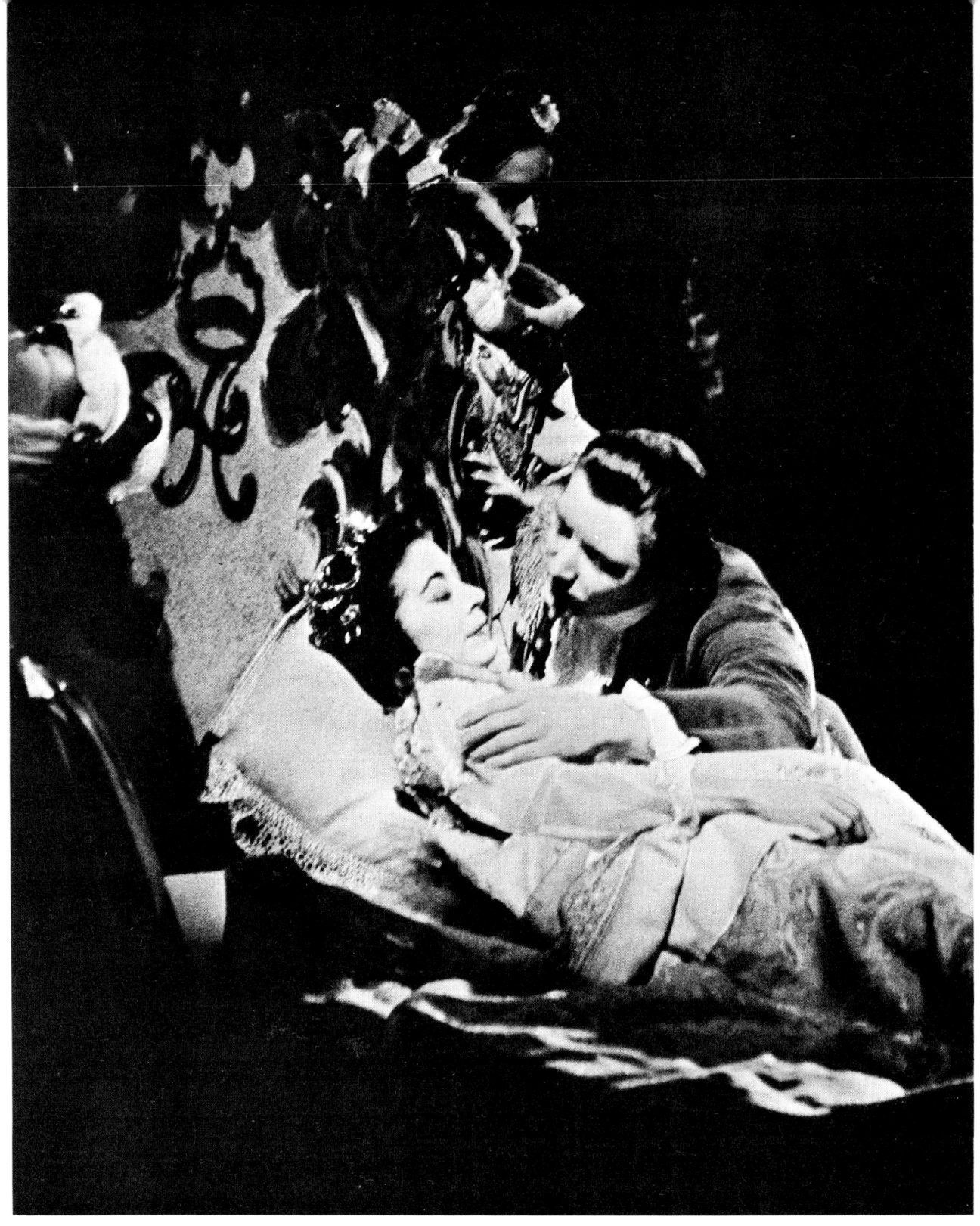

Aurora's awakening

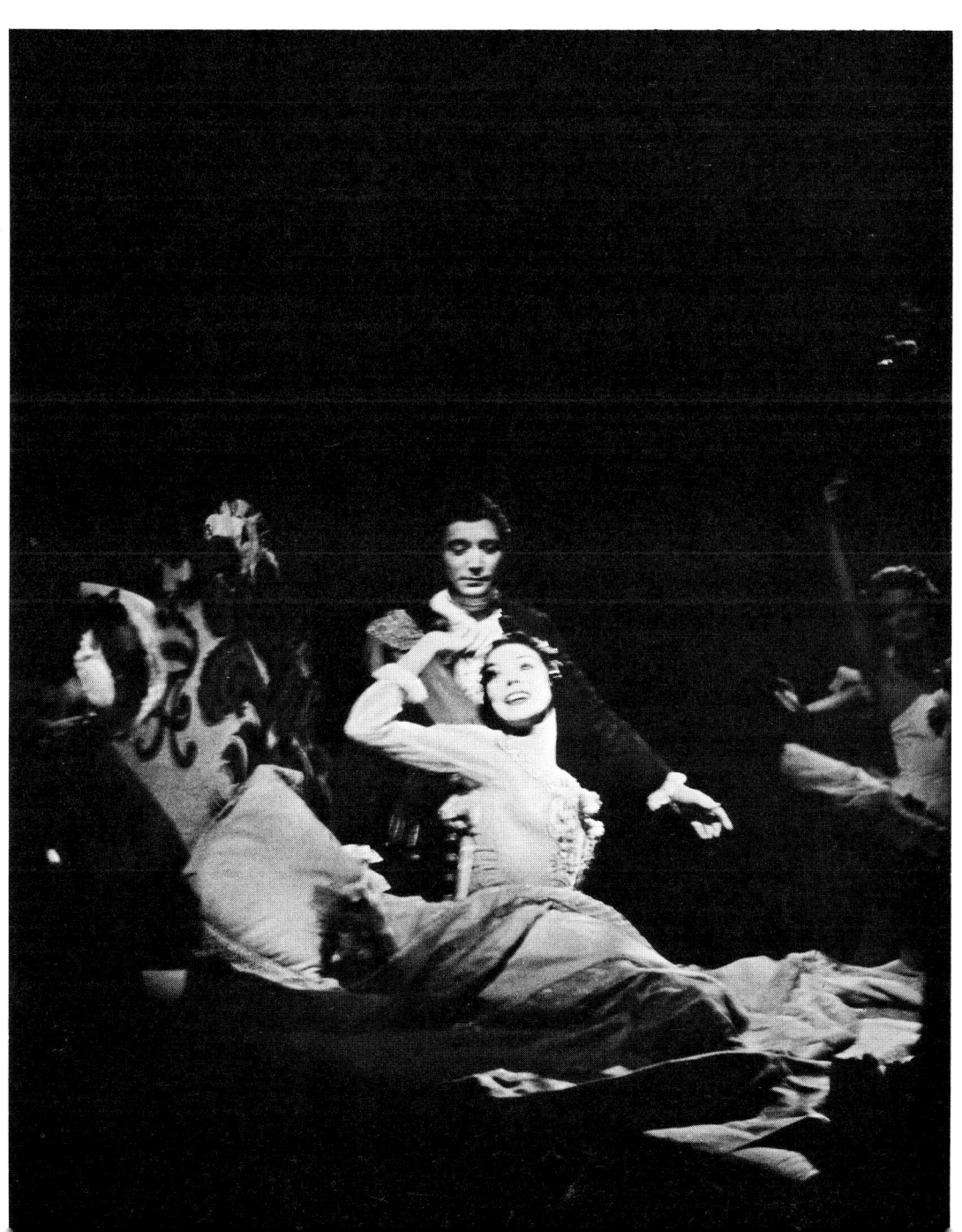

a "fish dive" during
the Wedding pas de deux
of Act III

Giselle

"I suppose I have seen more people do Giselle than I have the other classic ballets in my own repertory. Markova was my first great influence; she was my first influence for practically everything. Though I loved Giselle as a ballet I was very shocked, almost appalled in fact, at the idea that *I* should do Giselle. When the time came for me to dance it, almost two years had passed since I had seen Markova perform the role, but from my own memory, and from the memory of those around me, I tried to reconstruct the ballet exactly as she had done it; the thought of changing the slightest detail never entered anyone's head. One always tried to fill the previous mould, suffering from one's own inadequacy all the while. Giselle was such a contrast from Aurora; from the start I adored the whole ballet in a way that I never did with The Sleeping Beauty which followed. Giselle was a tragedy, and I think young people tend to identify themselves very readily with the idea of great tragedy. What was very difficult for me as Aurora was trying to act a 16-year-old girl when, in fact, I was only an eighteen-year-old girl anyway. There was hardly a question of 'acting' involved; I had to try to be almost what I then *was*, and that seemed to be far more difficult than any of the roles where I was required to act someone who was patently *not* me—like the flower-girl in Nocturne in love with a rich man who ignored her. All the dramas not in my real life were appealing to me then, rather than the happy teenager who was too close. I could not see where to start acting her; it seemed a vacuum. Giselle was someone with whom I felt quite close, though it was never considered to be one of my particularly satisfactory roles. I felt greatly the lack of models that I could study and learn from; my main inspiration at that time, and for years to come, came almost entirely from Fred, who would describe how various great ballerinas, such as Pavlova and Karsavina, approached their roles; how they actually danced. These suggestions of what others had done became vital; dancers really react most strongly to visual inspiration.

"It was a very long while before I dared any attempt to introduce hints of individuality into my shaping of the role. The mad scene was originally nothing more than a strict following of the pattern laid down by others; certainly in those early days one was told off roundly if one changed anything by even a hair's breadth.

(*right*) rehearsing with Rudolf Nureyev as Albrecht

Later, I started to try and develop the characterisation, and the period during the War forced one to develop; one was unable to repeat a ballet identically twice weekly—there had to be a search for new meanings. I very rarely *plan* changes though; they usually happen in performances. That is why I know there is such a great deal as yet unexcavated in Romeo and Juliet. It will excavate itself while I am doing it. In any ballet, a certain amount comes out in rehearsals for me, then when I start performances it is advanced one stage further. As I go on doing performances, in some strange way these things form

themselves. I never spend a lot of time thinking about the characters during the day; I cannot work in that particular way, but suddenly, during performance, one will come to some moment in the choreography—perhaps a simple arabesque or position. Then for the first time one senses a deep reason for that particular step; that she should, for instance, turn her head slightly at that point rather than look straight ahead. One suddenly knows more of what she would be thinking

at such a moment. The new discovery is added to one's performance, and this slight variation might then be retained for the next two years before it is discarded again. So many of one's moves are entirely instinctive that it is often dangerous if anyone tells one of particular moments that have 'worked'; one becomes over-conscious of their importance and the spontaneity is immediately in danger of being lost."

"Despite attempts to develop the characterisation, it becomes increasingly hard to present Giselle for the modern audiences, demanding, as they do, greater realism in the acting. This has always been the great problem for me, finding the narrow ledge between period Romanticism, with its charm and rather delicate pathos, and the reality of the situation where a girl goes mad with grief and shock and actually dies. To involve an audience in Giselle's tragedy one cannot go prettily deranged; one needs to go out of one's mind with utter realism. The great jump in style to the second Act is an enormous stumbling block; belief has to be suspended again. There is no hint of real logicality in the situation, lost as it is in a heightened Romantic dream. Audiences in the latter half of the last century could accept such fanciful situations, just as they could accept crumbling ruins at the bottom of their gardens—ruins which had been built by their own hands only a year earlier. Then again I feel that even within this difficult framework, not enough is made in the Covent Garden production of the struggle against the power of Myrtha as such; the desperate triangle seems blurred.

"My Giselle *has* gradually evolved over the years, but it is not one that I am happy doing more than three or four times a year. Certainly I enjoyed coming back to it again with Rudolf in the role of Albrecht. He seemed to have the great knack of combining realistic acting with the necessary heightened Romantic flavour, and to this one could respond. Also, he brought with him different ideas—how the Kirov worked with particular passages—so that there was a chance to view the situation afresh, in fact re-work the whole ballet again, just as I had done with Karsavina a few years earlier. Even between these violent re-appraisals there have been constant small changes—so small that very few people have noticed.

"What still worries me most about Giselle as a ballet is the long peasant pas de deux which intrudes into Act One and breaks the story. Giselle and Albrecht find it very hard to get back to the original sustained mood after it. People have forgotten about the girl who is suddenly running about losing her head. At one time during the War we dispensed with the peasant pas de deux, and from Giselle's and Albrecht's point of view the ballet was much more agreeable."

Giselle, feeling Albrecht's sword beneath her feet, crouches to grasp the cold steel

the death of Giselle

Giselle's spirit sustains the exhausted Albrecht during the dance of destruction demanded by Myrtha, Queen of the Wilis

Giselle pleads for Albrecht's life

"It never seems possible for me to sit down and complete the whole jigsaw. Each new piece adds to the design, but it is difficult to see the whole pattern; pieces tend to fall out, and then one has a constant urge to try others in varying ways. The moment a fragment loses its validity it must be dropped, even if it means one will never complete the whole design."

Albrecht is saved by daybreak which signals the destruction of the Wilis' power. In anguish, he carries the form of Giselle back to her forest grave

"I was helped enormously in doing my first Giselles by my partnership with Bobby Helpmann. He is such an innate person of the theatre that the experience of working with him proved invaluable. He showed me so much in the way of stagecraft and in fact forced me, in self defence, to learn how to claim one's own share of the stage. When I opened the door of Giselle's cottage and stepped out, it was to step into the *atmosphere* of Giselle. Bobby, on his first entrance with cloak and sword, had already made the audience sit up and participate; the atmosphere was already there for one in some uncanny way.

"In the early days I probably never said two words to Bobby off the stage. I was younger than he was and very much a junior; in fact rather frightened of approaching him in any way. But he was a very sympathetic partner and I felt perfectly at ease when endeavouring to create a performance with him.

"There is no doubt that he was the absolute star of the company in those days, the rest of us merely trailed along in the background. People do not seem to realise nowadays just how much British ballet owes to Bobby Helpmann. Even the crowds outside the theatre after a performance were very much greater than they ever are today. He was a magnet that held things together in a remarkable way. Just his humour alone was an invaluable asset during the war years, and with Fred disappearing into Service, Bobby's talents had to include the choreographing of ballets, as well as leading the company as a dancer."

A midnight discussion over stage management problems with Robert Helpmann. Athens, 1963

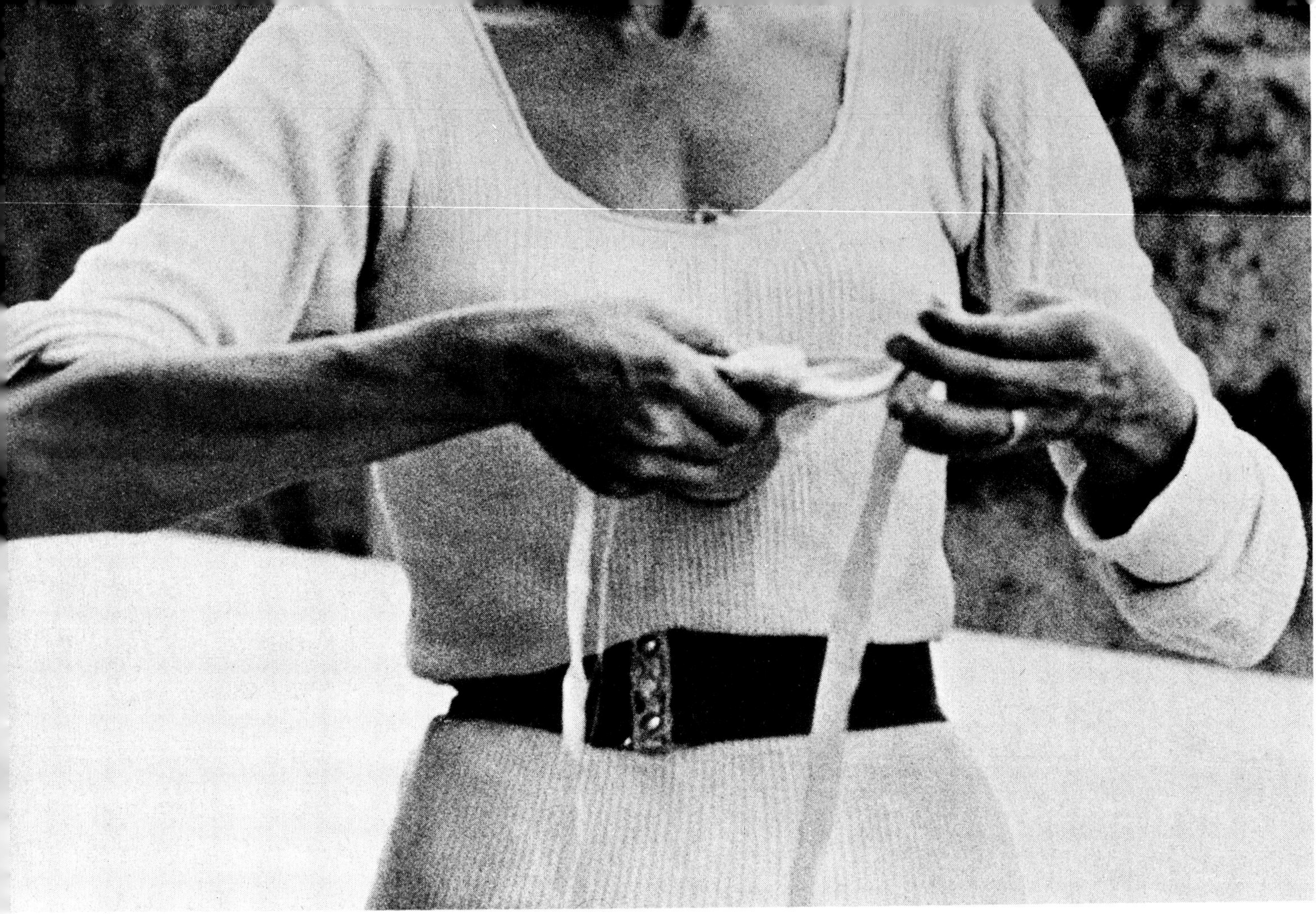

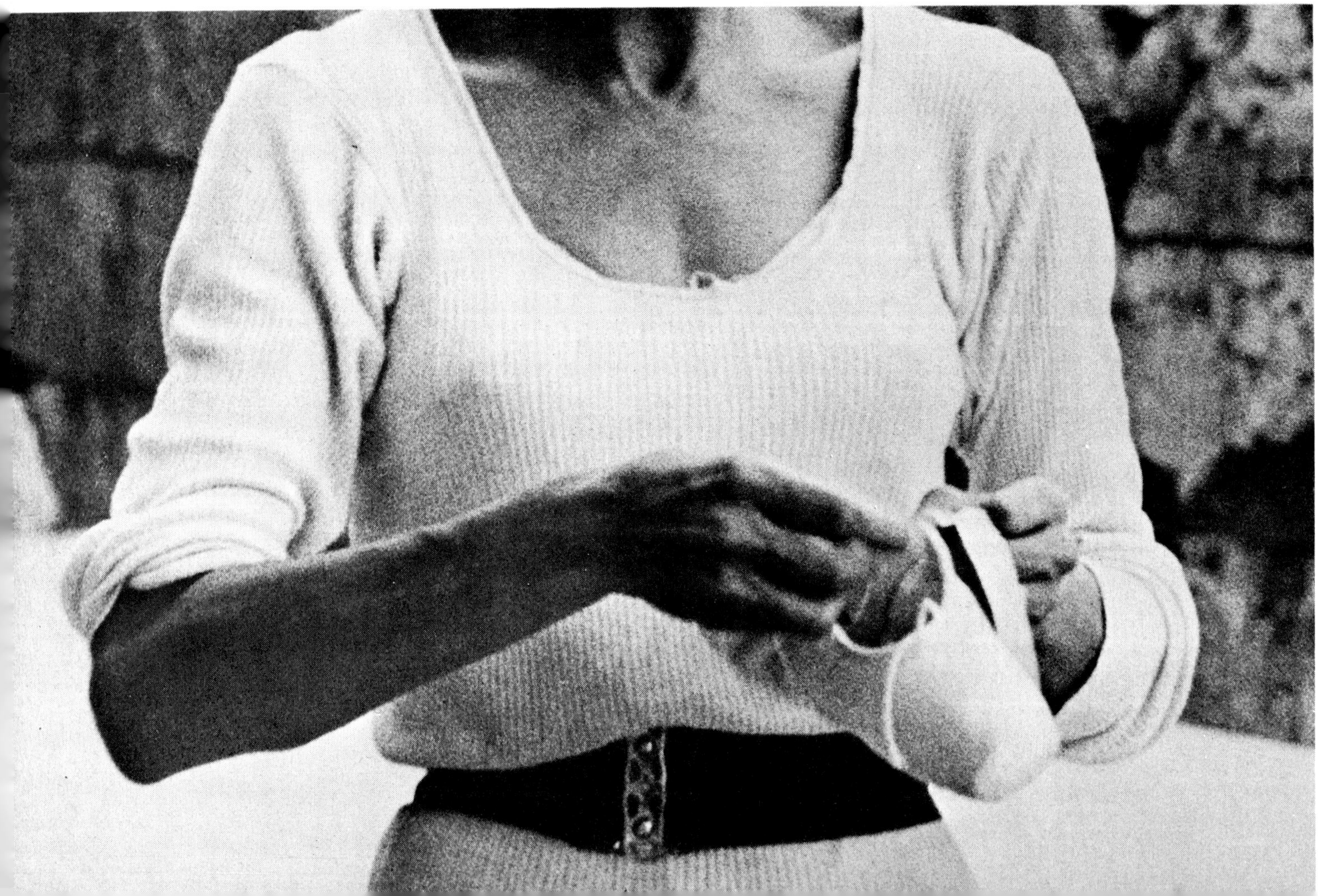

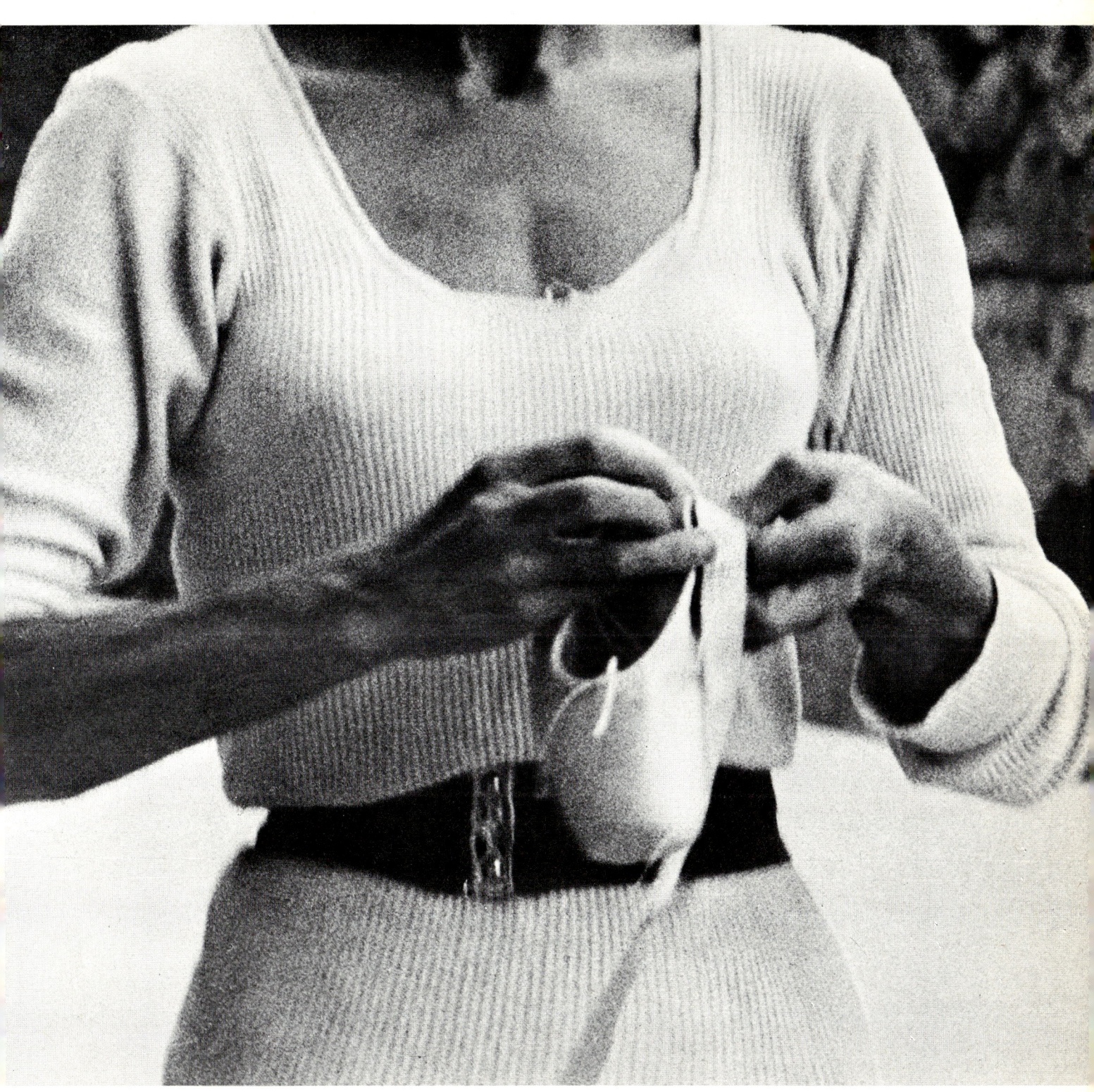

ribbon stitching—the eternal chore

"Physical disability of any sort undermines one's confidence so. It permeates every aspect of a performance unless one somehow manages to be very strong-minded. I'm sure if everyone knew how physically cruel dancing really is, nobody would watch—only those people who enjoy bullfights!"

Fonteyn's physical blessings have included perfect body proportions and legs which, while being highly individual among those of ballet dancers, could justifiably be called the most beautiful legs in dancing. Her feet on the other hand have never been strong and have been a constant source of nagging discomfort and worry. I recall her hobbling about despairingly one morning, showing me an alarming bump, and then suddenly declaring:
"It's no good—I shall have to put my feet in a gas oven!"

Symphonic Variations

"As a ballet structure, Symphonic Variations had to form a complete circle and end up where it began. When he first choreographed it, Fred matched much more incident to the music than now exists; there was much more there. But he was suddenly landed with extra time—something like three months—because of an injury to Michael's knee, so that although everyone was very happy with the ballet as it then was, we still continued to rehearse it, even on stage. Fred slowly eliminated every item that was not essential; that is why it is his most perfect choreographic work—he had the time to revise it. It was as though it became refined and purified to the essence. He spent a very long time pondering on the best way to end the ballet; and also solving the problems of all those chains crossing and circling, linking and breaking, then forming again. Most people seem quite prepared to sense hidden meanings in the ballet; Fred is always rather surprised at just how many things people do see in it. There is so much feeling in the music, and this he has interpreted. It is a measure of just *how* well Fred has choreographed it to the music that people can still extract from it any meaning they wish."

with Royes Fernandez,
Athens, 1963

"All those early ballets that one did with Fred had a special atmosphere—a special feeling; and for some reason we always knew what it was. We felt it; we knew and understood it. Not that Fred ever actually *said* anything, but if I think back to Nocturne and Apparitions and Dante Sonata there was a special quality present. Particularly, of course, in Symphonic Variations—because although it was apparently abstract, we still had a sense of this feeling beyond just the steps; some emotion—that one simply cannot express in words—exists in the choreography of that ballet.

"To me it means that Fred is a choreographer who *feels*, rather than just hears, the physical notes and bars in the music. He seems always to understand a 'line' in a phrase of music, something which has some relation to what was in the composer's mind. I find him the most musical choreographer imaginable; his choreography will take that long line in the music, unlike most choreographers who do each bar at a time, or each four or eight bars at a time. In those eight bars are all the various items that one can hear, and Fred might miss, or might get five steps into four bars, something which might not seem quite right—yet over 32 bars he has some extraordinary way of feeling the music. It is a special quality of his.

"Right from the start I always worked in that way. Somehow the *spirit* of the ballet and the music guided one. I never bothered very much about the steps in Fred's ballets, or whether they were difficult. It was never a question of that; one was always involved in what was being expressed, rather than with the mechanics. One simply did not think about the steps very much; one thought about the expression, the mood. Nocturne was a particular example. He had the atmosphere of that Delius music to perfection. Always it was the expression that was the vital ingredient. That to me is the great quality in Fred's choreography: the musicality which understands the feeling of the *whole* music. The pictures of Symphonic Variations taken in Greece are very happy in coinciding with the purity of this ballet.

"Sophie Fedorovitch's art was also an art of elimination. If something was not vitally necessary in the designs, then it did not appear. To me, Symphonic Variations is Fred's memorial to Sophie."

Hamlet

Fonteyn created the role of Ophelia in Robert Helpmann's Hamlet in 1942; her return to the role for two performances in Baalbek in 1964 was something of an occasion; it allowed one to admire afresh the unerring grasp she has for small ballets of style. The character of the role is filled out intensely, yet finely controlled and never allowed to overbalance the structure of the work. Helpmann's ballet concerns itself with the state of the dying Hamlet's mind:

> "For in that sleep of death what dreams may come
> When we have shuffled off this mortal coil,
>   Must give us pause."

Ophelia's few minutes on stage are a series of vignettes flashed in quick succession; visual sketches of states of mind.

"Hamlet was a splendid ballet for a small stage; it should never really be spread out in large settings such as the Opera House. A claustrophobic atmosphere is vital to its effectiveness. Once this is lost, the fevered intensity risks looking melodramatic and overblown; the mental thread is dissipated. I felt that Baalbek was an ideal setting for it. That immense, brooding temple loomed over one almost oppressively and, in a paradoxical way, concentrated our puny figures."

as Ophelia,
with Rudolf Nureyev
as Hamlet. Baalbek, 1964

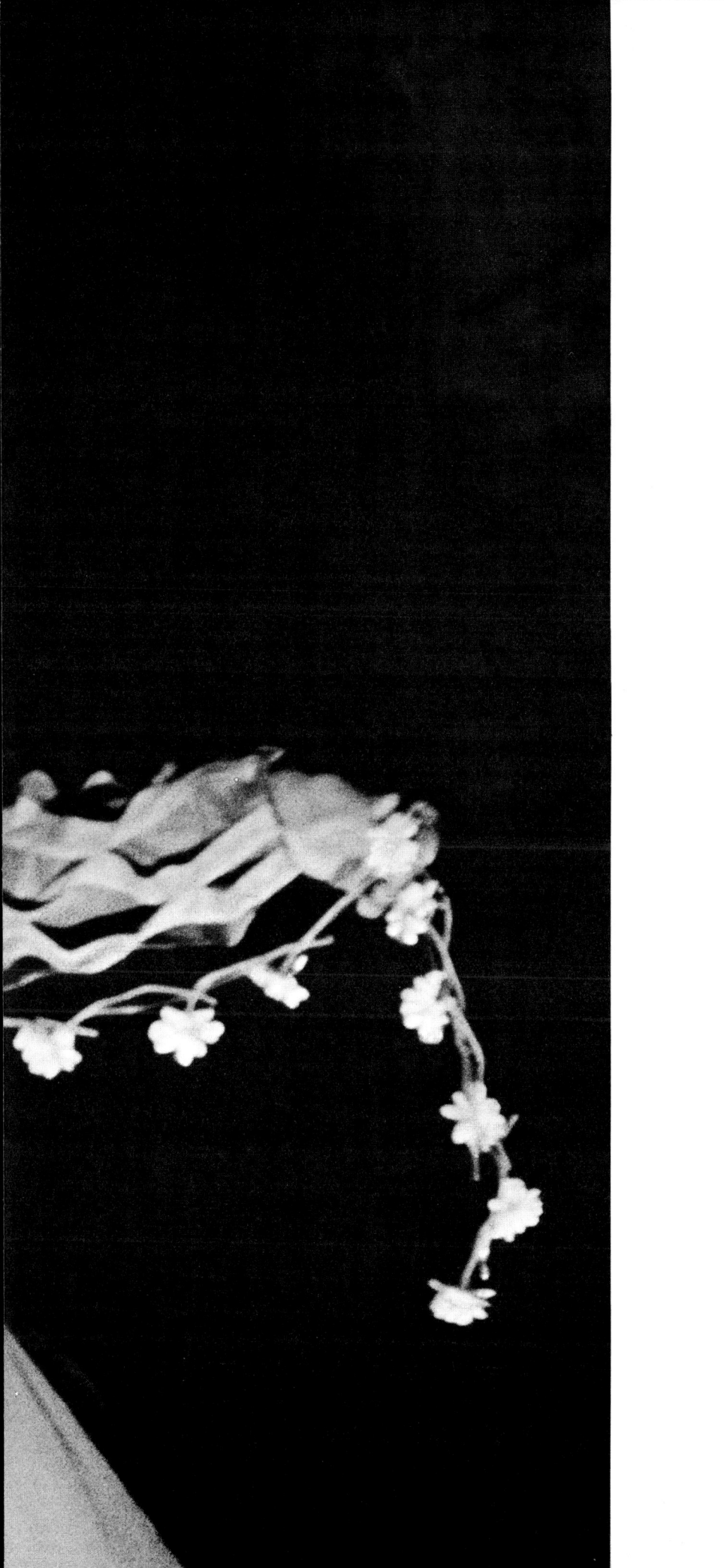

(*left*)
dancing with Laertes

In Hamlet's fevered brain, the ghostly images
of Ophelia and the Player Queen become blurred and confused

Swan Lake

"Swan Lake is so big in every respect. There is nothing one can say about it. To me, it has always been the most terrifying of all ballets. I think of it as the ballet world's Hamlet, in that it is virtually indestructible; it exerts a continual fascination, it survives countless versions all over the world, and it can provoke some response in people of every race. This in itself is remarkable, because the story—if one tries to examine it closely—is another of those wild illogicalities. I am not even sure if it is made clear in the programmes these days that Odette really does take on fully human form between midnight and dawn—all those feathers and flutterings tend to confuse the issue.

"I suppose it is the ballet in which I have least altered my views on the way it should be performed. I have had to dance so many versions around the world, yet the guiding aim has seemed constant. My performance has probably not altered very much since I first danced it.

"Just the steps alone are so extraordinarily difficult. If one succeeds in doing a performance of Swan Lake even fairly well, then one probably derives a greater satisfaction from that than from any other work one might do."

Fonteyn now realises that although she knows all her other characters as *people*, she sees her dual roles in Swan Lake as something entirely abstract. Even in roles such as Firebird or Ondine she has been clearly an individual spirit. Her Ondine, for example, is a particular ondine among ondines.

"Oh yes—I know her *very* well. She's a strongly individual ondine.

"I know all the others. I know Giselle very well; her friends; where she lives, the trees with the sun shining through the branches."

as Princess Odette in the Prologue

with Rudolf Nureyev in the role of Siegfried

Although Fonteyn made her debut as Odette in December 1935, and began dancing the double role towards the end of 1937, her guiding aim in Swan Lake is something which she herself hardly understands. This may seem odd, applied as it is to an artist who has produced one of the most complete and profoundly *sensed* interpretations of our generation, yet in another way it is probably the most essential answer of all. The spiritual abstraction which illuminates her Odette comes from a mainspring which is sacred, because it is not understood. When pressed to define her attitude to Siegfried; whether he appears to her as a singular individual or as a symbol, Fonteyn became aware for the first time that she does not in fact see the prince as a man; possibly only Man. The central core of the ballet is Love, a rock around which swirl all the forces of destruction. Its survival rests on it being of unflawed purity. Each pas de deux in the ballet becomes an expression of a universal truth, an aspiration or an ideal.

For her, the idea that she should have to go on in the Ballroom Act and remind herself that she has become the Magician's daughter as opposed to Odette, is almost an unnecessary confusing of the greater issue. The actual change of costume is the only solid, physical fact. Odile is an expression of Man's longing; a deceit clothed in desire, and intangible.

One of the many remarkable things about Fonteyn in this ballet is her indescribably subtle alteration in body line. Her Odette has a sorrowing curve at the centre of her line that is quite unlike the dancer in any other role. Along with the marginal ups and downs inherent in any dancer's work, Fonteyn's best Swan Lake performances have continued greater and greater. To see one of these performances now fully realised, is to be the privileged spectator of a complete masterpiece. Nothing can be added or subtracted. If Swan Lake is the Everest of classical dancing, then Fonteyn has seen the view from the summit.

rehearsing the balance from the Black Swan pas de deux

Odile dances with Siegfried in the ballroom

action photographs taken during 1964

rehearsing with David Blair for the opening performance of the revised production, December 1963

(*right*) with Keith Rosson as Rothbart

with the corps of
the Royal Ballet,
Covent Garden, 1963

"There is nothing so nice as lying naked on some deserted shore and eating cheese and drinking wine."

DAPHNIS AND CHLOË

Longus' classic Greek tale of the innocent love
between a goatherd and a shepherdess

Christopher Gable
as Daphnis

Chloë is caught between the pleasing attention of Daphnis and the unwelcome attention of Dorkon. Ronald Hynd as Dorkon

Daphnis and Chloë watch Dorkon's clumsy efforts in the dance competition

Chloë held by Dorkon during a boisterous game amongst the villagers

Daphnis is crowned
as winner of the dance
competition between himself
and Dorkon.
The prize is a kiss
from Chloë

"Daphnis and Chloë is probably the one ballet I wanted to do more than any other. Like many things in life, it happened that I had to show a great deal of patience in waiting for my wish to be granted. I knew the story even before I heard the music for the first time, so that my response to the score was immediate—it captured the essence of its subject so securely. Everything seemed to be choreographed effortlessly when the chance finally came to do the ballet after all that waiting. Each of my variations seemed to be worked out, with a brilliant off-hand casualness on Fred's part, in less than an hour, often in half that time. His genius was revealed afresh when we both went to Greece some time after the opening of the ballet. Everything was a miraculously true echo."

Daphnis and Chloë section photographed November, 1964

During a raid on her village, the terrified Chloë is abducted by the pirate chief Bryaxis (Alexander Grant)

SIR FREDERICK ASHTON

"When Margot was first pointed out to me as ballerina material I was unable to find much inspiration in her. I was conditioned to Markova's sharpness and precision in dancing and, compared to all that brittle delicacy and finesse, Margot was not impressive to me. She had weak footwork, and in some way she did not use her body properly. There was no doubt that she was the most promising of the young dancers at that time, but there seemed to be a constant tussle in all my early contacts with the young Margot.

"When finally I created for her the role of The Bride in Baiser de la Fée, I felt a great frustration in being unable to mould her precisely as I wanted. Her performance needed to be much more precise. I got very cross with her at times and went on and on at her, relentlessly. One morning after I had been particularly severe, she suddenly rushed and threw her arms around my neck and burst into floods of tears. I knew then that I had won the battle; that I would be able to work with her. From that moment we were never at real loggerheads again. Her technique, and particularly her feet, gradually strengthened as her tuition progressed. One was immediately aware of her innate musicality and her wonderful physical proportions. In addition to these gifts she had, even as a young girl, a considerable sense of line. In fact, with her particular proportions, it was very difficult for her to make an unpleasing shape. It was her line that I concentrated upon using most; that, and her very beautiful arm movements.

"Even as a young girl she was able to hold her own on the stage extremely well, and her partnership with Robert Helpmann was an unusual and interesting one. He provided the stagecraft and theatricality which she balanced with her lyricism. Of course she was very receptive and absorbed a great deal from him in the way of mechanics, but her artistic instincts and her discretion *never* went beyond her own correct artistic limits. She always had that great gift—which she displays to this day: a wonderful sense of measure. Never once did she make a gesture which was not completely true; one that did not come from the heart. Nothing was exaggerated. If her performances then were lacking in any respect, then it was because she felt unable to indulge in anything that she did not feel.

(left)
Chloë's humiliation in captivity is expressed in a
solo compounded of pleas, defiance and piteous despair

(*right*)
Chloë's joy expresses itself in a rapturous solo danced to the accompaniment of Daphnis' flute

"I remember once, after a performance in a role which she had been doing for at least two years, saying to her 'Well, at last you did that just as I have been wanting you to do it!' And she replied 'You see, for the first time I understood what you told me two years ago.' She had to discover the essential truth of it for herself. Certainly she did model her early performances in Giselle very closely on her predecessor, and this was no bad thing for a young dancer. I sometimes feel that young people tend to react *too* violently against the example of elders. Those old Ballet Masters had a reason behind so much of their work. It is no use discarding that unless you can replace it with something better. Even in the most severe technical passages there is some theatrical 'occasion' to be discovered. I tried to impress upon Margot right from the start that there was a great drama to be found in the Rose Adagio for instance. That one must take classicism and make it live afresh through oneself; otherwise it becomes a dead thing. Her early performances as Aurora were very fine, but nothing more than a sketch of what was still to come. It grew and improved constantly.

"One of the many rare things about Margot is her ability as an actress; she is marvellous in this respect. I remember a great lady of the theatre remarking once 'We learn more from coming to watch her than we do from many of our own people.' Margot has an *effect* on the public. Along with her other attributes she has a feminine warmth which readily communicates itself to an audience. Even as one of six performers in Symphonic Variations she was, on the one hand, able to submit with perfect ease to being an equal player in a sextet, yet within this context she still dominated the ballet and gave the clue to the performance. If that appears to be a negation then it is only because it is a positive negation. For that reason, if for no other, Symphonic Variations might be one of the greatest things she has ever done. It means that she never misses the measure. Because of this she was also a great comedienne in the days when she had more opportunities to display this aspect of her work. Her sense of humour *is* very marked; also she has an instinct for what the French call the 'accident du Théâtre'.

"Although the young Margot often had to follow Markova's example, I certainly do not see in her any echoes of the latter. In fact I do not see echoes of anyone else in her work. She is individual. It would be true to say that there is a similarity of approach between Fonteyn and Karsavina; both marvellous actresses with enormous range. They have both been great Rep. dancers too, rather than someone like Pavlova who was one of those dancers who tend to exploit their own personality. To my way of thinking, the great repertory dancer is greater than the great 'individual' dancer. Margot embodies lyricism carried to its fullest degree, and lyricism is certainly an English characteristic. But because of Margot's international validity, it is difficult to describe her within the close confines of being *English* as such. America really saw her blossom internationally. It was a tremendous test, but she rose to the occasion as she always does. Then, she knew the challenge, and she had the courage to accept it in that first performance of 'Beauty' in New York. They could not help but respond to her own personal beauty, as well as to her precision of line. There appeared to be no effort involved in anything which she did; there was no pushing. Also, on that occasion she brought forth a tremendous theatricality which one had never seen in her before. It was as if she rose out of herself.

"Even so, one cannot be great without brains; she has plenty of those! She possesses great heart, compassion, sympathy and loyalty. In the early days she was like a delicate plant; one that needed continual feeding and watering. Our work together gradually became a dual thing. I had an instrument to work with, so that the progression was mutual. We fed each other in this artistic partnership; it was a case of the right elements being in the right place at the right moment. Had I not been able to work with Margot I might never have developed the lyrical side of my work. As it was, it evolved into a personal idiom.

"Margot is a person who cannot be hurried. When we moved to the Opera House at Covent Garden after the War, I noticed with some disquiet that her effect was not registering fully. It was because everything which she had done in the small theatres had been seen so much quicker in those more intimate conditions. Effects take longer to register in a large theatre. I walked about all over the Opera House, watching her during a rehearsal. 'It's no good,' I said, '. . . you're not registering!' Suddenly, she held a position a moment longer than normal, and I shouted 'This is it!' And it was. She filled the theatre."

Chloë is restored unharmed to Daphnis, after the intervention of the god Pan

"It is so easy dancing Chloë; everything just happens."

Photographs should at all times explain themselves readily, yet in the case of the picture above, one is tempted to elaborate on the essence of truth in Fonteyn's line as it is here arrested. Daphnis lifts Chloë six times above his head, rising with the tide of music. Her arms float alternately above her head, and the effect is of an exultant jet of water rising and falling at the centre of an elaborate fountain. Here we see the perfection of shape in Fonteyn's arm; the curve in this instance is the curve of a column of water as it turns and responds once more to gravity.

"Daphnis and Chloë are children sprung from the land and nurtured by it. Their innocence is pure because it is natural. Their feet have been in constant touch with the raw earth; with their hands they scoop the water to drink."

At the wedding dance which concludes the ballet, Daphnis carries Chloë aloft, in and out of the patterns formed by the celebrating villagers

Frederick Ashton was inspired to match the luminous Ravel score with one of his most exquisite ballets, and the breathtaking perfection of Fonteyn's Chloë—possibly her very greatest creation—remains one of the unforgettable art images of a generation

The closing scene of Daphnis and Chloë

Ondine

There is a flash of light as a form settles like an idling minnow caught in a patch of sunlight; and then one is aware that she *is* there—still, breathing softly, her arms telling of water weed as it yields to the current. The creature (for one hardly thinks of her as being human) peers wide-eyed through the veil of the waterfall at the shadowy castle courtyard. Tentatively, one of her arms ripples through the cascade, to hover for the span of one heartbeat before the cool night air startles it back to its own environment.

Thus, even before she has fully revealed herself in the dimensions of the stage, Fonteyn has unerringly caught us in a web of credulity concerning this water sprite Ondine. We know she is a water sprite not so much by her appearance as by the fact that the air dried the moisture of her skin during that first darting exploration, and we felt it too, as surely as if a moth had just brushed its wings across our own fingers. Truth. Truth of feeling expressed through movement in space.

"Chloë's innocence is a human innocence;
Ondine is innocent in a different way,
for she has no knowledge of the
perfidy and deceits of Man.
Her being is too direct and simple
to absorb such nuances of emotion."

"Oh, that stupid shadow; it makes me so angry!"

with Michael Somes rehearsing Donald MacLeary in his role of Palemon

"Many of our ideas about the characters in Ondine changed as we continued to work together. Fred would suggest something to us, but as Julia, Michael and myself continued to rehearse we would sometimes find the characters taking charge in ways we never intended. Fred never interfered unless he thought something was actively wrong."

Sir Frederick also stresses the curious independence of these characters:

"Ondine had been in my mind for a long time. When I knew that I had to find a big ballet to do for Margot, it was Ondine that came to the fore. The only difficulty was that I had always visualised Ondine as a blonde—possibly because of the famous Rackham illustrations. In the event, Margot's darkness seemed to intensify the role to advantage; it became stronger and fuller than it might otherwise have been. Many of Margot's characteristics *are* in Ondine, but even in my mind the character—in fact all the characters—kept taking charge and developing on their own, often when I least expected it. It was as if they controlled their own life."

(*left*) The choreographer watches a rehearsal of one of the shadow dance sequences. Ondine's shadow is joined mysteriously by a second set of independently moving arms. She is unaware that Palemon is behind her.

two moments in time, with an interval of 24 hours between them...

La Bayadère

The famous last Act, The Kingdom of the Shades, from the historic four-act ballet, entered the Royal Ballet repertory on November 27th, 1963, reproduced by Rudolf Nureyev. He played the role of the Indian warrior Solor, searching for the spirit of his beloved Temple dancer Nikiya, whom the Rajah Dugmanta has had put to death by a snake in order that Solor might marry his daughter Gamzatti. Solor is haunted by the beautiful Nikiya as he dreams of the strange kingdom.

Though the Minkus score is an uninspired servant to basic balletic rhythms, the Petipa choreography has a finely woven clarity worthy of Bach. Fonteyn's very pure and precise line makes her eminently suitable for the role of Nikiya in this white Act, and she is one of many famous dancers who have had successes in the role; others have included Kshessinskaya and Pavlova at the beginning of the century.

La Bayadère photographed during performance, 10 March, 1965

CLASSICAL FOUNDATIONS

At the age of six, Fonteyn was receiving her earliest dancing lessons in England. Her good fortune was in her teacher, a qualified instructor, clever with children, and one who entered her pupils for the Royal Academy of Dancing examinations. She had the gift of a personality which could make her charges enjoy their work. More than this, she was able to explain the correct fundamentals of classical schooling to Mrs. Hookham, who thereafter took care during the family's travels in America and China, that her daughter would take lessons only from teachers who showed a similar approach to schooling.

"Sometimes I was at a particular school for only one week. My mother would sit and watch and, applying what she had understood from that first teacher in England, decide whether or not the teaching was beneficial or harmful. It was usually the classes which I enjoyed that proved to be the ones we never returned to! My mother would say quite calmly 'We won't be going back to that school next week,' and the job of finding another class would begin all over again.

"From an early age I accepted dancing classes as part of my life. In China I was taking lessons two and three times a week. In Shanghai, between the ages of twelve and fourteen my classes were daily. Under Gontcharov, a Leningrad pupil, I came to understand that dancing was more than just a collection of dry exercises."

Back in England in 1933, she studied daily under Astafieva. "To my mind she was a very great teacher because of the way she could always indicate precisely *what* one had to do to make a step work. She made difficult technicalities seem possible. She was a fascinating person. When she died it was a great loss to me—I adored her."

1934 saw Fonteyn entered in class at the Sadler's Wells Ballet School under Ninette de Valois. Her strictest training had begun.

"My first solo role was the Young Tregennis in The Haunted Ballroom—a role I took over from Freda Bamford. I didn't have any steps to dance at all. I was always quite happy acting around the stage; it was the steps that made me nervous... as they still do."

"One cannot place a sufficient value on great schooling. During a performance I can still become fascinated if I catch sight out of the corner of my eye of the way in which Rudolf will place a foot on the stage."

pictures taken during barre work at Baalbek, 1964.

Fonteyn's back is probably as near perfection as one could find. It always reminds me of a plant stem; straight, pliant and with the subtlest of curves carrying the head.

Raymonda

In the summer of 1964, Rudolf Nureyev mounted the Kirov ballet Raymonda for the Touring Section of the Royal Ballet, and choreographically it proved to be an endless cascade of brilliant and inventive classical dancing. The premiere took place at The Festival of Two Worlds at Spoleto in Italy, but Fonteyn's debut as Raymonda was delayed by a call to her husband's bedside in England. However, when his condition improved, she was able to fly back and fulfil the last part of her engagement. Her appearance as Raymonda, so eagerly awaited by the Italian audience, took place on the final day of the Company's visit to Spoleto, with the exquisite interior of the Teatro Nuov packed to extreme capacity.

The enormous exactitude of Raymonda's role and the desperate strain of the previous week were menacing clouds immediately dispelled as the ballerina made her first entrance. Radiating an almost incredible assurance, she accounted for the first allegro solo, and its gathering of the flower posies, with an exhilarating perfection. Her mastery of the ballet and its style continued triumphantly throughout the performance. The memory of Fonteyn's last Act Hungarian solo—all shimmering, drifting bourrées, and lit with an intensely aristocratic inner fire, is unforgettable. The whole company took light from this performance and were worthy sharers of the final, prolonged ovation as they stood proudly behind their great ballerina and her partner.

(*left*) rehearsing in Spoleto, with Rudolf Nureyev as Jean de Brienne

as Raymonda, in Baalbek, Lebanon

THE BIRTH OF A BALLET

A widely publicised highlight for the Bath Festival of 1964 was Kenneth MacMillan's choreographing of a new pas de deux for Fonteyn and Nureyev, to music by Bartok. This was to be played by Yehudi Menuhin, organiser of the Festival. Rehearsals for this new work were strictly limited, owing to the pressure of engagements for all the parties concerned; indeed it transpired that there were just four rehearsals in all before the dancers left for a season in Australia commencing in early April.

Plans for further rehearsals in Stuttgart during the dancing engagements there during the latter half of May fell through, so it happened that every step of creation in this work fell under the eye (and camera) of the recorder of this book. Thus, the record presented here is probably unique, capturing as it does the entire creative process between artists, from the moment when five disparate personalities first assembled in a rehearsal room on a bleak winter's morning.

Other factors conspired to underline this unique condition. Late during the evening prior to the first performance at Bath, the news was received of the shooting of Dr. Roberto Arias during a political incident in Panama. Fonteyn spent a sleepless and distressed night receiving hourly telephone reports on her husband's condition. The news in the early hours of the morning seemed encouraging, and the ballerina was urged by those speaking to her from Panama on her husband's behalf to delay leaving for Panama until after the performance that evening. Early in the morning the worried Festival authorities and a large Press assembly were told that the ballerina had made the decision to undertake the evening performance before driving to the airport.

The theatre was closed to the Press for the final rehearsals and performance, with the result that the latter pictures in this section constitute the only existing record of the ballet as costumed. After a nerve-racking day both artists performed flawlessly in the evening, creating such prolonged enthusiasm in the audience that the whole work was encored. The second official performance of Divertimento never took place; Fonteyn remained in Panama by her husband's side. Here then, is the brief life span of Divertimento.

FIRST DAY

A Saturday afternoon. The large studio at the Ballet School is cold and bare. Rain splatters the windows, blurring the view of leafless branches patterned against a flat grey sky. Fonteyn and Money come into the studio simultaneously. Fonteyn does barre work while conversing. Ten minutes pass before Kenneth MacMillan enters. He is wearing a half open black zip suit and fawn leather slippers, and is clutching a recording.

MACMILLAN: "Hello."

MONEY: "Well, you *must* have been pleased with 'Images' last night!" (Images of Love, MacMillan's latest ballet at that stage, had received its second performance the previous night.)

MACMILLAN, smiling: "Yes. . ."

FONTEYN: "Everybody's saying it was a wonderful performance. Anyway, you *look* happy; you've got beady bright eyes!"

MACMILLAN: "Do I? Well yes it was very good. . . I feel absolutely wrung out though. All wobbly! (*He does a wobble.*) Is Donald coming?" (Donald Twiner is the pianist for the rehearsals.)

FONTEYN: "Yes, he's coming along."

MacMillan takes a seat, lights a cigarette, then examines a set of photographs of Images of Love with quick, nervous observation. His only comment comes at the end: "There are some very good ones."

At this point Nureyev enters, silently. He commences barre work immediately, remaining silent. Finally he begins to acknowledge other people's presence with his eyes, turn by turn. He wears a black sweat shirt with long sleeves and unusually neat fitting dark blue tights. He looks surprisingly fresh and relaxed, despite a late night after a Hamlet performance.

Donald Twiner enters, carrying a book of music and a portable electric fire. This he plugs in near the piano.

MacMillan: "All right. Let's hear a bit."
Twiner plays seven bars; all single chords. He repeats it. MacMillan puts down his cigarette, placing it carefully across the cigarette box lying on the floor by his chair. He gets up and takes Fonteyn and Nureyev to the centre of the room. "All right," he says, taking Nureyev by the shoulders. He stands closely behind the dancer, then marches him forward across the room to the count of seven. Fonteyn watches and then repeats the movement, taking MacMillan's place. It is a simple walk, with a turn to the left, half way along, and one to the right on the final count.
Fonteyn: "Shall I step sideways on the turn?" She moves accordingly.
MacMillan: "Yes—that's nice." There are some more bars of music from the piano. MacMillan listens intently. Everybody waits, still. Eventually the choreographer puts down his cigarette carefully, gets up, and tries a slight goose step on his own, counting. With his hands, he emphasises the rise on the ball of the foot. The music continues to be flatly harmonic.
MacMillan: "It's very strange!" He asks for a repeat of the opening bars. Fonteyn steps neatly behind Nureyev, concentrating.
MacMillan: "Hands up, here, Rudi. (*And by way of explanation:*) He's looking for her. . ."
Nureyev: "Ah!"
MacMillan: "The first time you did that, Margot, you somehow got behind him at a sharper angle." She tries again.
MacMillan: "That's better." He gets up and experiments with some turns to link on to the end of the entrance march. The two dancers try

them several times. Fonteyn has to experiment more than once to get a satisfactory effect.

MACMILLAN: "Now we'll sort out the feet! Arabesque at this point I think, Margot. A final turn on the seven." He demonstrates on his own. Twiner plunks a sustained chord which allows MacMillan to count a full seven.

MACMILLAN: "Rudi, you could match Margot's line at this stage?" Nureyev tries, but it does not come easily.

FONTEYN: "I'll get into *his* line?" She tries. It seems to work. Twiner plays the next few bars. MacMillan sits concentrating, staring at the floor ahead of him.

Finally he puts his cigarette down on the box on the floor. He tries for several moments to balance the cigarette and prevent it rolling, before getting up, leaving the cigarette to roll on to the floor. He advances quickly to the others, then stops and thinks. There is a deep silence in the room. The cigarette smoulders quietly. At last he demonstrates a step. Twiner plays the next few bars. After an array of the by now almost monotonous chords there is a sudden, unexpected trill. Everyone looks up at the piano, startled, then laughs.

MACMILLAN: "Comes as a surprise, doesn't it!"

FONTEYN (laughing): "That's where a mosquito bit him!" Nureyev tries a snatch of singing, improvising on the trill.

MACMILLAN: "All right; we'll do all that bit again.

(*There is a backward jump for the dancers on the trill.*) On the mosquito..."

('The Mosquito' is now destined to be the balletic catch-phrase for this particular point in the music. It serves as an identifying tab.)

Twiner plays; comes to the trill again. Nureyev suddenly mimes some frantic fingering—as a guitarist, yet one somehow 'sees' that the instrument is a violin!
NUREYEV: "I could play too, no?" He mimes.
FONTEYN: "Yes! And I'll hold it!" She bends down, pretending to hold a violin by each end. Nureyev plucks an imaginary pizzicato on the imaginary violin with his pointed toe. Curiously enough, it looks incredibly deft. There is general mirth. Finally, they repeat the previous few steps.
MACMILLAN, to NUREYEV: "Remember you're looking."
NUREYEV, groping humorously: "Sort of 'Where's the music?' (*And in a despairing tone*) Where's the music?"
MacMillan watches them try the sequence once more.
MACMILLAN: "It seems agonising, doesn't it! Actually it doesn't look too bad. I know it *feels* quite awful, but it's coming along. I keep thinking 'It's about time we started some dancing; it must be half way through!' Then I find there's about another ninety pages!! . . . . Shall we stop here?"
TWINER: "You've only got four more bars to the end of Section One." Nureyev goes over to look at the musical score.
NUREYEV: "Where are we?" Twiner points—it is only the second page. Nureyev lets out a squawk, then plays a few notes himself, reading from the music. MacMillan experiments with some more steps, this time with the two partners separated on either side of the room, though doing the same steps. Nureyev has some difficulty timing the actual steps. MacMillan watches him.
MACMILLAN: "You step on the *three*."
NUREYEV, comprehending: "Ah!" He tries it several times.
MACMILLAN: "All right, let's stop. Ten thirty tomorrow."
Everyone disperses with remarkable speed, forgetting to turn out the lights. It is still raining.

SECOND DAY

Sunday Morning. A clear blue sky. Money arrives, followed by MacMillan. The others are all late in varying degrees. After Donald Twiner's arrival there is a longish wait for Fonteyn. She creeps in. While everybody waits for Nureyev, Fonteyn begins stitching her shoes and asks Twiner to play the music of the first section. She walks through the choreography, waving the needle dangerously near her face during some of the arm movements. Twiner repeats the music. The ballerina stitches and thinks.

At 11 a.m. Nureyev enters, looking rather ruffled and sleepy. There is more barre work and general warming up, with a conversation about the critics in the Sunday papers, and their views on Images of Love.
MacMillan: "The Telegraph says I've choreographed myself dry."
Nureyev: "And the Express?"
MacMillan: "They don't. It's Sunday."
Fonteyn does a deep arabesque. One of her hip joints 'plops' with an alarming noise. Everyone laughs.
Fonteyn: "That's better! It's warmed up now."

They start work, going through the whole of the first section rehearsed the previous day. Everything goes without a hitch until the final steps, which Fonteyn muffs very slightly, biting her thumb as soon as she realises she has missed the timing.
Nureyev: "Margot, what are you thinking about when you do that bend? Are you thinking about turning, or about bending?"
Fonteyn: "Do I *have* to be thinking about something?"
Nureyev: "You are not turning easily. . ."
Fonteyn: "It's my feet. . . They get in the way somehow."
They repeat the movement under discussion. It appears satisfactory. Donald Twiner plays more of the stark music, all single chords.
MacMillan: "Sunday morning music! All right. From the silence, Donald."
Nureyev, laughing: "Play silence!"
MacMillan: "From your mosquito. . ."
They repeat the section. The final individual steps of the section still seem tricky; the timing is very subtle. MacMillan gets up and walks them through a further section. They try what he has shown them.
MacMillan: "That's not bad actually—just let me see it again."
He goes over to Fonteyn at the conclusion of the move and experiments, holding her leg while he promenades her in arabesque. Nureyev then tries the movement. MacMillan does not like it. He re-designs the move, with a support behind the shoulders and under the arms. Rather surprisingly, the new section of the piano score introduces a warbling cadenza. MacMillan listens, fingering his lip and nodding almost imperceptibly at the floor while he concentrates.
MacMillan: "Let's have one of your kooky steps here." He takes Nureyev by the sleeve, then demonstrates a sideways movement with strong undulations of the arms.

FONTEYN: "Is that for both of us?"
MACMILLAN: "Yes."
TWINER, watching them: "Want to make that a nine? It will be seven, eight, *nine!*"
MACMILLAN, to FONTEYN and NUREYEV: "Once more, from the three. The 'leaning' three."
They repeat the squiggly arm movements and the sideways walk. Twiner strikes two more notes, calls: "E - *lev* - e - en."
Fonteyn looks up. "That's half way through!"
TWINER: "Yes, exactly. It's the bottom of the page. He (Menuhin) goes yarrummph! 'I'm half way through!'"
MacMillan pulls a punch-drunk, cross-eyed face.

MACMILLAN: "Now—one of those sleep-walky walks." He moves about the floor. "Up, down; creepy, crawly; side, side; creepy, crawly; up, down!"
Fonteyn and Nureyev copy the movement without much difficulty, until the last step.
FONTEYN: "I've forgotten the up, down." She looks at Nureyev and then at MacMillan. "Rudolf finished with the music, but *I* finished early, because I did what you told me."
MACMILLAN to NUREYEV: "Do it by yourself."
NUREYEV: "Oh." He bites his tongue and begins.
MACMILLAN: "He's finishing on the eleven, actually, I wanted it on the ten. If you *can* finish on the ten, because I want you to look at each other on the eleven."
They repeat the steps, then turn inwards towards each other, Nureyev with a mock ferocious stare on his face and Fonteyn with her head on one side peering into her partner's face with the look of a quizzical bird.
MACMILLAN: "I think we should try and remember the things we've done! I'm absolutely baffled. Lost!"
They repeat the whole section, from beginning to end. MacMillan watches, taking an occasional puff from his cigarette. When they finish, he says: "Shall we walk it from the beginning?"
FONTEYN: "From the *beginning*?"
MACMILLAN: "Yes." He watches it all again, then puts a hand over his eyes. "It's very strange! *Very* strange!" There is general laughter.
FONTEYN: "It *feels* like the music."
MACMILLAN: "It's getting very kooky, this— for Bath!"
NUREYEV: "That's why they want it."
MACMILLAN, to FONTEYN: "Which way are you going to do the rond de body?"
FONTEYN: "I just go which ever way I'm pushed."

They repeat the circular movement of the two figures locked at arms' length, with a friction movement of the interlocked arms. It makes everybody laugh. Fonteyn scratches Nureyev's shoulder comically, with her index finger.
The movement is left to work itself out later.
MACMILLAN: "I think we'd better do something straighter now—after all that scratching."
NUREYEV, looking up at the window: "Aaah! (*Sadly*) All the beautiful weather's gone."
MACMILLAN: "Perhaps we'd better end there for today."
There is a general discussion about further rehearsal times and costume fittings before everyone leaves. The lights are left on again.

THIRD DAY

FONTEYN to TWINER: "Did you make those two notes?" (She is referring to a point in the score.)
TWINER: "Yes."
FONTEYN: "Recently—or a long while ago?"
TWINER: "Just this minute!"
FONTEYN: "Oh. I always miss that. I think I was very tired that morning (*hand to forehead*). It didn't go into the IBM machine properly! Now it's coming out wrong—like the machine in Canada that gave away too many students' scholarships. It's somehow better if I don't count and don't listen—just keep going in a trance."
MACMILLAN: "Yes, much better."
FONTEYN: "If I count, I can't hear the music, and if I get nervous I forget to count! Then I'm really lost."

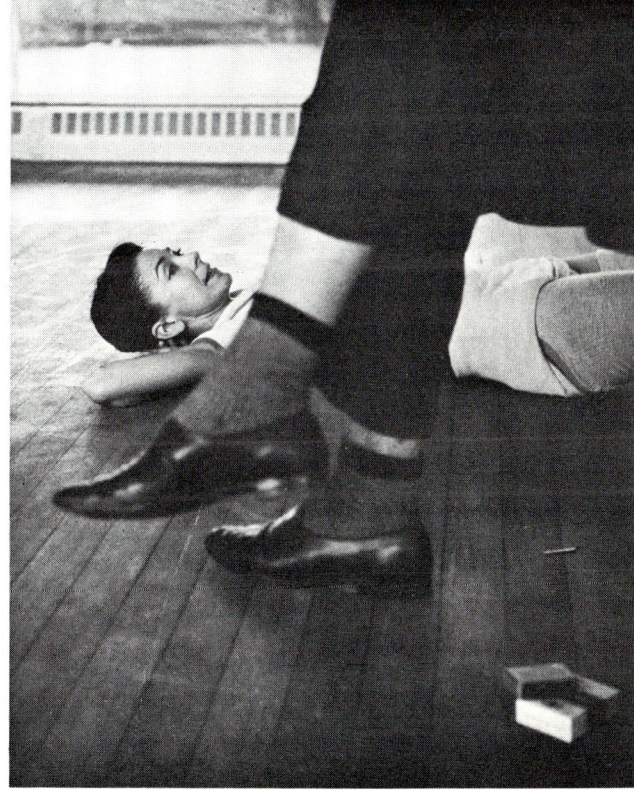

Nureyev has entered and has watched the last few steps. He goes through his section and in the process 'discovers' a step which has been lost. There is a general chorus of "Aha!"
MacMillan: "How did we manage *without* that?"
Fonteyn: "We managed *perfectly* without that!"
MacMillan: "No wonder you had trouble getting out of that arabesque, Margot!"
They begin again from the beginning.
In a satisfying way the whole thing
'falls together' with neither partner making
a mistake.

FOURTH DAY

As usual, the work begins with a reiteration of what has gone before. During a pause, MacMillan lights another cigarette and comments: "Someone telephoned me this morning and asked 'Was it all finished?' I went ha, ha, ha—very lightly."
He watches the two dancers as they repeat the previous section once more, then he says: "We'll go on. Now what's next?" Twiner plays the new section. MacMillan exclaims: "That's going to be *impossible* for us to count! It's triplets, you see; it's all mixed up!" He looks resignedly at Twiner. "Play it again . . ." His face crumples like a squeezed lemon. "Uuuugh!"
Fonteyn's expression is compounded of amusement and resignation, but she says nothing.
MACMILLAN to TWINER: "How do you suggest we do it?"
TWINER: "Count it very slowly."
MacMillan gets up, then looks around at the dancers. "What foot are you on? I never remember!" He demonstrates what he has in mind. Fonteyn and Nureyev repeat it without difficulty.
MACMILLAN: "*Now* what happens?"
TWINER: "Then there's an eight." He plays. MacMillan experiments with an arabesque for Fonteyn, and follows it with a backward pull.
FONTEYN, biting her lip: "I'm not sure. . . ."
MACMILLAN: "No. I'm not sure either."
FONTEYN: "I'm going back now. Let's go back." She begins alone, then pauses presently. "Something syncopated—only I can't remember what it is." She tries again as MacMillan watches her feet.

MacMillan: "Ah—yes! Let's go back.... same place again." He remembers the link. After remodelling the arabesque for Fonteyn he looks across to Nureyev, who nods that he has understood. A solitary mug of tea has been brought in. MacMillan looks at it reflectively, then asks Twiner: "How much more have we got?"
Twiner: "Another four lines."
MacMillan: "Play it."
Twiner: "What—the whole four lines?"
MacMillan: "Yes."
Nureyev sits cross-legged on the floor nursing the tea and listening. MacMillan experiments with an exit walk as Fonteyn stands watching him in the mirror. Both dancers then repeat it with hardly any prompting, and at the second attempt they complete the whole final section without a mistake. The basic structure has been accomplished.

Incident with a deserted tea-cup

but when she got there, the tea-cup was bare . . .

First theatre rehearsal, Bath—June 8, 1964

Morning, June 9, 1964
The shock of the news received the previous
evening from Panama produces a mental pressure
which causes terrifying lapses of memory

Designer Barry Kay
supervises adjustments to
his costumes

Afternoon:
Kenneth MacMillan walks Fonteyn through a difficult section

Divertimento *pas de deux in performance*

Yehudi Menuhin
plays the solo violin
accompaniment

Marguerite and Armand

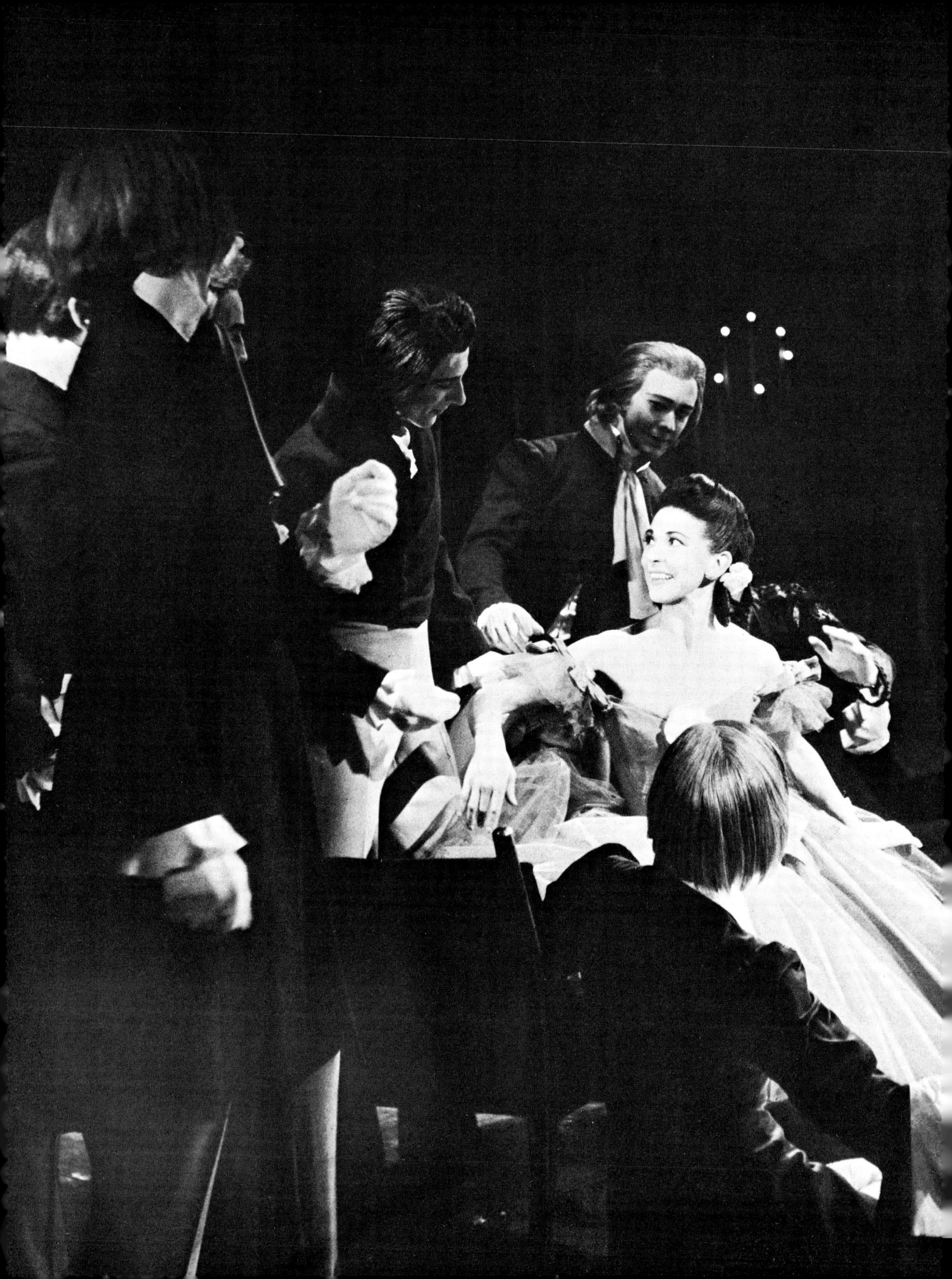

Marguerite and Armand sequence photographed during performance, 22 March, 1965

Frederick Ashton's ballet—a condensed version of La Dame aux Camélias—is told in a series of intense and poignant flashbacks rapidly succeeding one another. The work is a starring vehicle in the grand tradition, and as such it has allowed Fonteyn to prove herself one of the really great Marguerite Gautiers of the theatre

THE
FIRST
MEETING

Rudolf Nureyev as Armand

IN THE COUNTRY

Michael Somes as Armand's father

THE INTERVENTION

THE LAST
MOMENTS IN
THE COUNTRY

Marguerite, fatally ill, returns to the protection of the Duke (Leslie Edwards)

ARMAND'S
INSULT

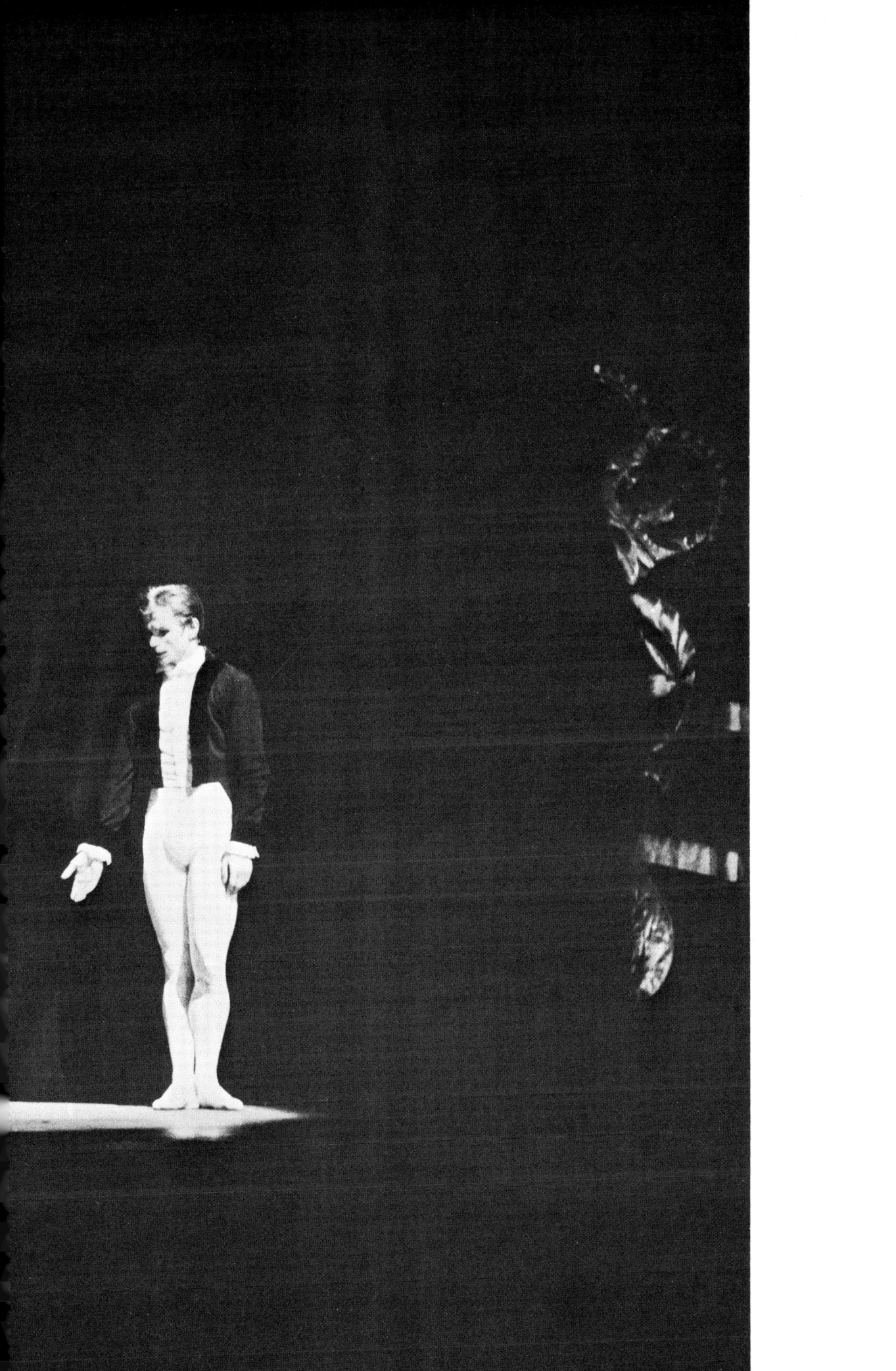

as Paquita, during one of the annual Benevolent Galas organised for The Royal Academy of Dancing by its tireless President: Dame Margot Fonteyn de Arias

DAME NINETTE DE VALOIS TALKING WITH KEITH MONEY

K.M.: "What were your first impressions of Margot the pupil?"
de V.: "The first time she came to the school I was struck by her great talent and equally struck by her numerous faults—which I knew had got to be put right. She had had tuition everywhere, and it had been of rather a free order. Now here was an extraordinarily gifted child who, for the first time, had to come to terms with a strict routine of work. It was hard for her, as she had not been subjected to anything like it previously. Her potential talent was offset by this undisciplined approach to work; she had never had to submit to the control that her particular physique required. She had, luckily, an extremely sensible mother, who supported me very strongly over my attitude towards Margot's lessons and the form which the tuition would have to take for some time.

"It is a fact that one of the first remarks I made about Margot was: 'I think she has arrived just in time for us to save her feet.' She was not even standing on them correctly; they were in a terrible state. I remember that I made her change her make of ballet shoe, and that is something that any dancer of any age hates to do. Margot was no exception to that general attitude! But she was an extraordinarily intelligent child, and even where her temperament was in opposition to the routine and discipline, her intellect was definitely prepared to submit. There was a fight going on within herself and I could sense it, for it is possible to sense such a struggle in young people, and it is a very good sign. One does not want 'Yes' pupils, but there is of course a moment in time when the 'No' pupil has got to be won over somehow. This was at the root of the trouble that Ashton had with her at the beginning. He once volunteered the remark 'I don't see anything in her.' It was understandable, for she was very unpredictable due to her vague undisciplined technical background. The everlasting changing of schools in various countries had left her, naturally, with no solid foundations, and it was this weakness that Ashton could not, at first, get beyond. He was unable to see the practical

another Gala role: in Ashton's Birthday Offering, first performed for the 25th anniversary of the Royal Ballet

reasons (understandably, because he wasn't teaching her) for the basis of the trouble. That was my department, and it was all too clear to me. Nevertheless, it was slow work for a while.

"Yet I was always aware of this very rare jewel and treasure: a young girl who, when won over, was one of the most incredibly loyal, hard-working and dedicated of dancers. She had found her roots at last in England. Previously she had been a very rootless little person, for the parents had travelled a great deal and she had travelled with them. I do think that such children lose something in their youth, although of course there is much that they gain. In Margot's case her nomadic life had most assuredly sharpened her intelligence and her appreciation of things, but for an adolescent it had become an existence without much aim and purpose.

"It isn't necessary for me to talk about Margot as an artist. One instinctively knows that here is greatness. The Italian ballet master who trained me, always used to say that a ballerina has got to have some highlight in her work. I must say that until the advent of Margot I had always agreed with him, but when you meet complete perfection, you don't know what is meant by looking for a particular highlight. Margot's greatness lies in her general perfection more than in any individually significant highlight. I don't think such special trappings belong to the really great. There is something more subtle about these people and Margot comes under the category of those who have this peculiar subtlety of quality.

"Of course she is exceptionally musical; musicality though is not just a highlight in an artist's work. It is the most important proof that there exists co-ordination of a rare order. Certainly it is not a mere highlight—not within the usual meaning of the word at any rate."

K.M.: "When Markova departed, and you knew that you had a very short space of time in which to find a prima ballerina, did it worry you that you would have to work so intensely hard on this individual? The astonishing thing is that there was an individual who had it within her to be a prima ballerina; presumably, in the final analysis, they are born rather than entirely made."

de V.: "No, it didn't worry me unduly. She was not so very young, you know. When she first danced Giselle she was seventeen. She was no younger than

Baronova or Toumanova. Margot did not work as hard as they worked, for they were, after all, in a fairly rough touring company travelling all over the globe. Margot had stability in this respect. We were stationed in London and only danced once a week at Sadler's Wells. It was anyway a very young company. Margot was not challenged—not in the way that a young girl is challenged today when brought out at Covent Garden. Ours was a very small company playing to a very specialised audience in a very private part of London. In some ways the conditions were ideal for her, particularly as she was a reserved, nervous and shy adolescent. I often wonder whether, if Margot had been in the circumstances of a very big company, she would have done as well at the start. I rather doubt it. She certainly had no severe competition, for there was no-one with her particular qualities. With her extreme sensitivity it was perhaps just as well that the path was a quiet one. I did discuss her dancing The Sleeping Beauty, very carefully with Sergueyev, who was a very wise old man. Naturally, with his background, he knew a great deal about dancers. He said that she could dance it. He said that he was quite sure there was nothing to worry about. Then again she was nineteen, which is not really so very young. Some of the conditions then were very much better for a girl who had to be developed fairly quickly than they are today. The time I really worried about

her was during the War. One worried about them all, but one particularly worried about this wonderful dancer, with the strain of dancing conditions at that time. I don't think the *pre*-War time was such a strain.

"Margot is an extremely sympathetic and wonderful person to work with, and she has intense strength and courage underneath this facade of reserve. The obstinacy which people so often mention—I don't think it is really as strong as they suppose. I think it is because she is such a very gentle, understanding person that when you do find she will not accept something, it is more of a shock than one anticipates. I don't find that she is really stubborn. I think, though, that she has convictions; and I would say that her convictions are very strong and when not fully and clearly expressed can give an impression of obstinacy."

K.M.: "Personally, I cannot really put into words what I feel about Margot; it would run the risk of being highly coloured, but I must say that in many respects I feel as strongly about Margot as I do about anyone in this world."

de V.: "Well, you see, greatness has this effect on people. I would say that in temperament and character she is very like Karsavina, of whom you were talking earlier. I have often noted this resemblance."

K.M.: "Margot has such astonishing range. How is it that she hits so faultlessly to the centre of so many diverse roles?"

de V.: "Everything about her is in complete proportion and such people have a very wide range of expression. Her talents are tremendously diffused. Dancers of strong highlights but whose talents are not so diffused, get 'type-cast'. The wonderful thing about Margot is that she has never been 'type-cast'. Naturally she is a great lyrical dancer, and in a ballet like Ondine she gives us something out of this world as a performance. Yet I find her last scene variation in Daphnis as great as anything she has ever done, and it is also one of the most glorious pieces of choreography that Fred has ever composed."

K.M.: "It makes me very happy to hear you say that. I suppose Daphnis and Chloë has always been the one ballet I have believed in more than anything else. That flute solo is so unbelievably perfect as performed by Margot, that one is really bereft of words. And rightly so. One cannot dare to try and describe it."

de V.: "Yes, it's incredibly lovely."

K.M.: "There is always one phrase tossed about very casually in ballet circles: 'Of course she is not a great technician.' To me this is a tiresome and irritating remark, quite apart from being inaccurate. From a purely analytical and critical point of view, has she in fact gone on developing her technique over the years?"

de V.: "I call her technique very sound. She's no virtuosity dancer—that is something quite different. A question of these highlights again. She is not a virtuoso, but she has an extremely neat, accurate technique in my opinion. I would regard her work on the whole as exceptionally tidy and beautifully placed. After all, line, placing, precision, phrasing, control—everything comes into technique. And there is a state of perfection there, which is what technique means. One hides technique, one doesn't display it as such. Definitely Margot's technique is hidden in the apparently effortless perfecting of every movement she does."

K.M.: "I suppose it would be wrong to label her as an 'English' dancer in the parochial sense. . ."

de V.: "Well, I don't altogether agree. Margot has a great deal of the quality of the English School, which is famed for its all-round work far more than for its highlights. That was one of the things they noted about us in Russia. They said there was to be sensed an all-round feeling for detail and the importance of perfection in all general movement. Margot has that, and it does happen to be an English quality. In many ways her basic discipline and perfection are of the English School."

K.M.: "I certainly feel that she is a template for English dancing, but I have no way of knowing if I am wrong or right."

de V.: "This approach of hers—this 'thing'—is very English. Our dancers are reserved; nothing is projected just for the sake of projection."

K.M.: "She has a wonderful quality of equal partnership with *all* the people she dances with. . ."

de V.: "Great artists never dominate a scene or another artist. They create an atmosphere that is shared with a true sense of equality—which is quite a different thing. There is a difference between a great artist and a great star. Star quality can be a very dominating affair. There is this curious diffusion about Margot. I feel she diffuses her greatness as an artist on the stage in every way."

(*left*) as La Sylphide
in an extract performed
for an R.A.D. Gala.
A fortuitous hint of
the original Taglioni
lithograph here

K.M.: "I find that in certain roles she can be intensely, *immediately* moving; I also feel that in some roles she has a way unlike that of some other instinctive artists who also work from the heart. They make their impact directly from the heart, outwards. She can control it and channel it from the heart through the brain, and *then* out."

de V.: "As I said: she diffuses everything. . ."

K.M.: "Yes—it's a very deep and subtle factor. It has a wide effect. It took America by storm, didn't it?"

de V.: "She had a tremendous success there."

K.M.: "Before that first tour to the States, were you worried about the American reaction to Margot and to the Company?"

de V.: "Yes, I *was* worried. But the one thing I impressed on all of them was not to think of what American dancers did, or what an American audience would be looking for. I begged them to dance just as themselves—an English company. They would either be liked or not liked; there was absolutely nothing to do about it. I explained that the disastrous thing for them to do would be for them to try and meet something half-way without really knowing what it was they were trying to meet. I said they must present themselves without effort. Now it happened that that was exactly what America was prepared to accept—particularly in Margot's case."

K.M.: "And Russia?"

de V.: "It was a very big success there too, and Margot had a very big personal triumph in Ondine."

K.M.: "How did they react to Firebird?"

de V.: "I think they felt it was their ballet really, which is understandable. I think they were also slightly embarrassed that they hadn't done it themselves. But Ondine was a very big triumph."

K.M.: "She has waited a long while for Juliet. . ."

de V.: "Well, at one time she was very averse to dancing the role. Then she changed her mind. She has these bouts of uncertainty. I have known her not to dance a role for some time. As an example, she once came out of Lac des Cygnes for nearly two years."

K.M.: "One of the things which strikes me about Margot in Swan Lake is that her body takes on a different line from that body in any other role. There seems to be the most extraordinarily subtle, sorrowful curve inside everything she does as Odette. I can see her shape in every aspect of that role, yet I cannot take that shape of hers and fit it onto her in any other role. This, to me, is a rather startling discovery. I don't think it is purely imagination; in fact I know it isn't."

de V.: "Well, I feel sure that it comes from her extreme intelligence. Her understanding of a role shows through her body in movement. Contemplate, for a moment, a painful extreme: let us take a person who is a mental deficient. If you are as used to movement as I am, you can recognise the mental state of such a person just by watching them move. Movement is a very tell-tale way of showing up what is going on in the mind. At the other end of the scale, the perfectly tuned mind should speak faultlessly through the body. Margot's body is a wonderful servant to her acute mind and sensitivity."

Gayaneh

rehearsing an extract from Gayaneh with Nureyev: Athens, 1963

rehearsing Le Corsaire in Washington, 1965

Le Corsaire pas de deux
photographed during
performance at the
Inaugural Gala
for President Johnson.
Washington
January 18, 1965

Rudolf Nureyev
as The Slave

Sylvia

the leader
of Diana's
Huntresses

with Attilio Labis as Aminta

Covent Garden June 1965

Romeo and Juliet

Kenneth MacMillan's ballet to the Prokofiev score was premiered at Covent Garden on February 9th, 1965. There followed 43 curtain calls for this striking work. Fonteyn danced Juliet to the Romeo of Rudolf Nureyev.

"Juliet's peculiar brand of innocence is such a difficult one to strike at all accurately. One senses seething under-currents in that small, rather fetid provincial town, all of which must have had its effect on a vital young Italian girl. Despite her cloistered and protected life, she would be prey to continual servants' gossip. Also, the desperate importance which her parents place on wealth and social position would lead Juliet to sense a shifting world of false values. This background must be almost entirely responsible for her later actions.

"For me, Juliet and her family are so *very* real that there is still an enormous amount to be explored in that role; I feel I have hardly begun."

with
Rudolf Nureyev
as
Romeo

rehearsing the Bedroom
pas de deux

Gerd Larsen as The Nurse

In the Ballroom, dancing with Paris (Derek Rencher)

Juliet's first meeting with Romeo in the Ballroom

from the pas de deux
beneath the balcony

The secret wedding takes
place in the chapel of
Friar Laurence (Ronald Hynd)

The bedroom pas de deux

Juliet's parents threaten to disown her if she refuses to marry Paris

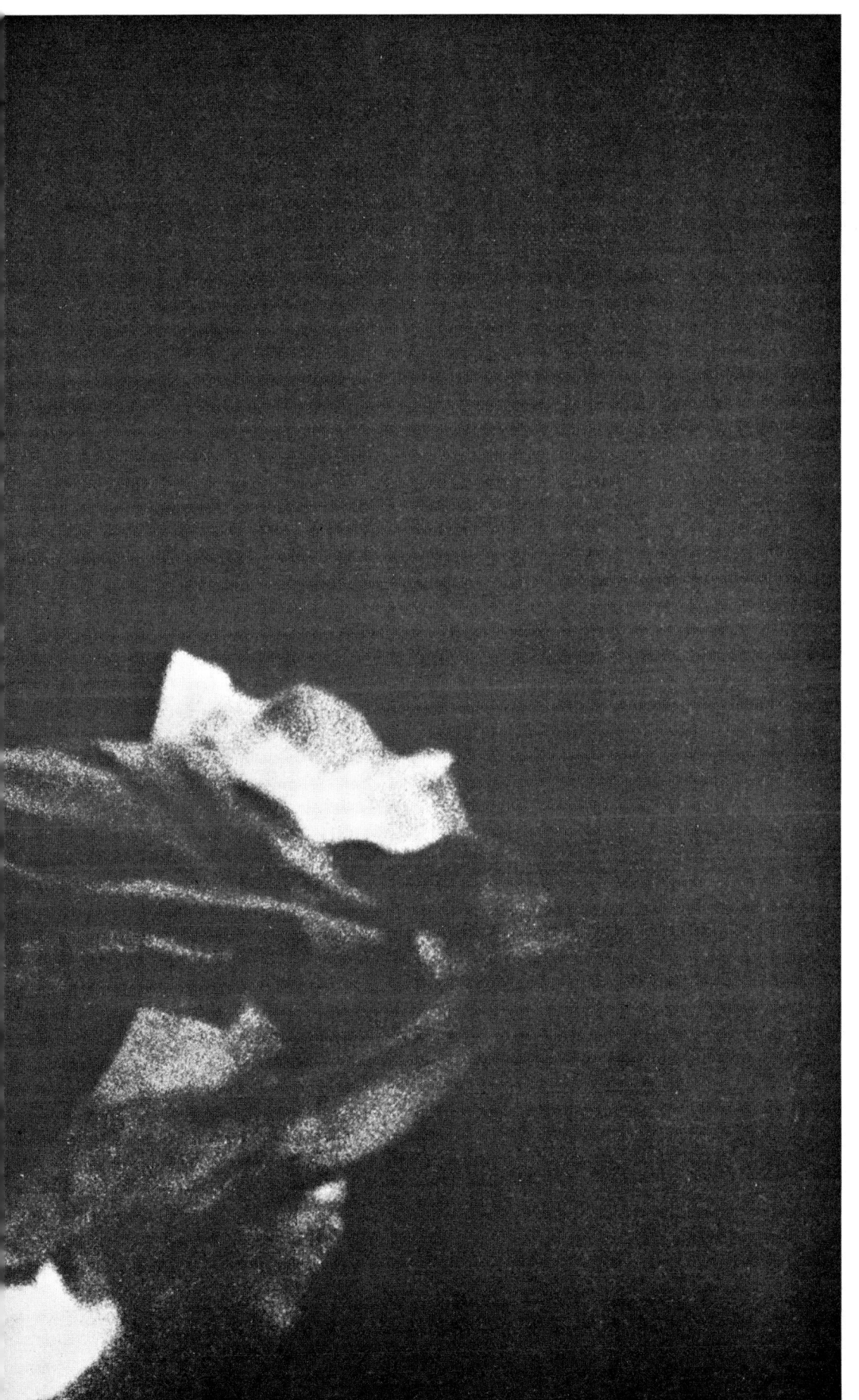

In desperation, Juliet flees to Friar Laurence

Juliet takes the phial
of sleeping draught given
her by the Friar

Awakening in the tomb, Juliet discovers Romeo lying beside her bier... and realises that he is dead

With the fatal knife that has already stabbed Paris, Juliet takes her own life. In the few moments that are left to her...

. . . she tries desperately to reach the body of
Romeo, barred from her by the cold stone

The effort is too great for her ebbing strength. Unable to raise Romeo's head sufficiently, she just manages to transfer with her fingers a final kiss to his cold lips

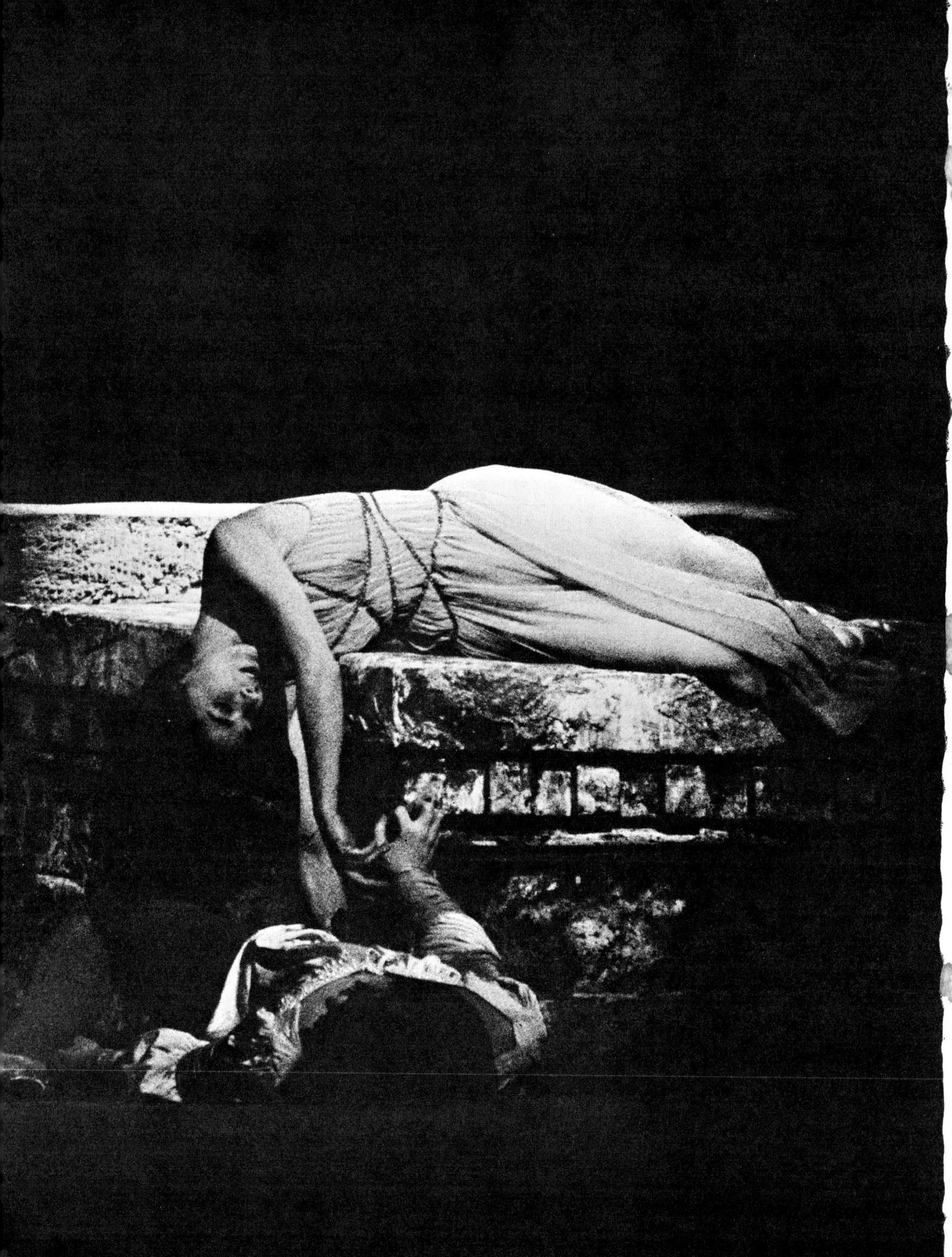

Opening night
of Romeo and Juliet
in New York
Metropolitan Opera House
21 April 1965